Marianne Paulossen

(1973)

STITCHERY: ART AND CRAFT

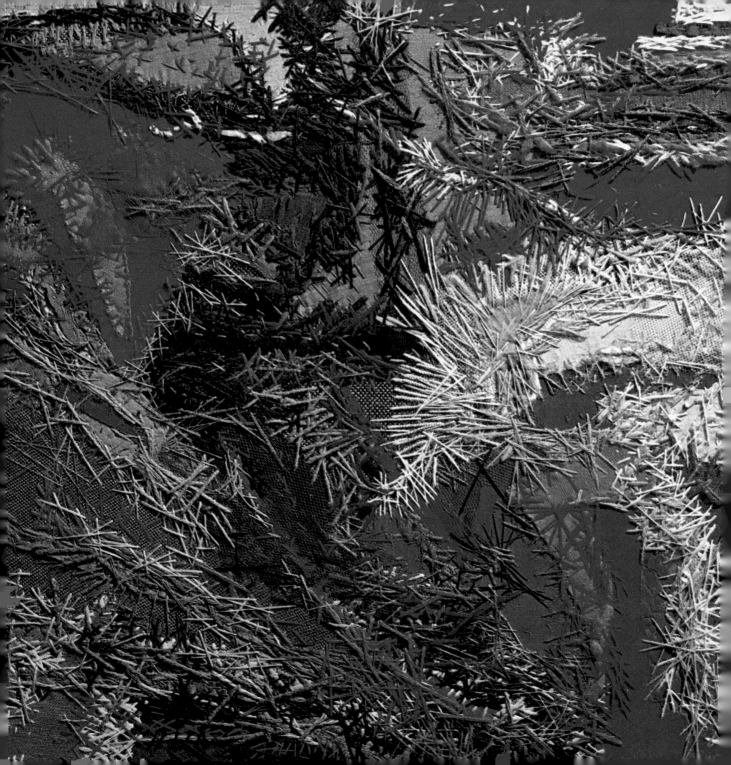

STITCHERY: ART AND CRAFT

Nik Krevitsky

An Art Horizons Book
Van Nostrand Reinhold Company
New York Cincinnati Toronto London Melbourne

Landscape: Flower Garden
Stitchery by the author.
(Photograph, Peter Balestrero.)

To the inventor of the needle whoever he may be, for making
the art of stitchery possible; to all who have used this
invention to aesthetic ends; to the artists who are exploring
new uses of this invention; and to the teachers who are the
channel and the bridge for future work, this book is dedicated.

Also by the author:
Batik: Art and Craft (Van Nostrand Reinhold)

VAN NOSTRAND REINHOLD COMPANY Regional Offices:
New York Cincinnati Chicago Millbrae Dallas

Van Nostrand Reinhold Company International Offices:
London   Toronto   Melbourne

Copyright © 1966 by Art Horizons, Inc.

Library of Congress Catalog Card Number 65-19678

Design Consultant: Milton Glaser
Type set by Graphic Arts Typographers, Inc.

Published by VAN NOSTRAND REINHOLD COMPANY
A Division of Litton Educational Publishing Inc.
450 West 33rd Street, New York, N.Y. 10001

Published simultaneously in Canada by
VAN NOSTRAND REINHOLD COMPANY Ltd.

16 15 14 13 12 11 10 9 8 7 6 5

CONTENTS

Foreword

In the current crafts revival needle arts have taken a position of dominance. Do-it-yourselfers find prepackaged kits and thousands of stamped designs available for their use and addiction. At a time when sociologists, among others, constantly remind us of the need to develop rewarding leisure time pursuits to counteract the pressures of modern living, it is obvious that a simple, clean, easily-picked-up, easily-put-down activity such as needle work would be tried by an increasing group.

The person concerned only with the busy-time aspect of the craft, interested only in making things for the sake of doing and of the things themselves rather than in the personal gratification of completing a unique conception, ends up with satisfaction based only upon the skill of the craft and of the relief of the completion of the work. Thousands, however, reject the product somewhere along the line because of monotony inherent in this activity. Alleviation of the monotony of routine tasks in contemporary living is one of the incentives of crafts for leisure pursuits. The crafts, therefore, must enhance rather than destroy their purpose in life. If the activity were to include the more personal involvement of

conceiving, planning, and designing, as well as executing, the total experience would be richer and more rewarding, the individualism or the personality of the practitioner more a part of the work. At any rate, psychologically it would be fulfilling on a level other than that of the completion of another's work, another's concept. Plato said that a slave was a man who got his purposes from another. The freeing of the needleworker from an attitude of enslavement is the aim of this book.

Ways of beginning for the insecure novice, ways of expanding for the already skilled technician, ways of appreciating for the consumer-observer are suggested in the approach used here. The child, fresh, spontaneous, unfettered by clichés and stereotypes, approaches this medium directly and with startling frankness of expression. If he is allowed the security of the courage of his aesthetic or intuitive convictions, no problems are likely to arise. If, however, false standards are imposed he is more likely to encounter stumbling blocks in the process.

The adult has another problem. Jaded by the bombardment of visual images in his environment and the clutter of images in his memory and subconscious he often

feels inadequate as designer-craftsman and frequently resorts to the convenient. He compromises on the packaged kit or the stamped design because it is so easily available and because it gives him a feeling of confidence. Its completion gives him a feeling of satisfaction, though the object is never really his.

This volume does not presume to be all things to all people; it does not show individual stitches or steps of learning them. There are many excellent sources for that information, and some are listed for reference. This book is directed to all beginners, to teachers, and to professionals as well as amateurs. Its intent is to present a broad array of work in the field at all levels; to introduce the curious person to a variety of approaches and design potentials; to present to all a panorama of work being done today in a medium as old as the needle and as new as the vision of the creative person of tomorrow. It also shows stitchery in its relation to other visual arts in the main stream of today's activity. It is the sincere hope of the author and the publishers that this concept of stitchery today will be of help to those who come within its reach and that it will introduce a stimulating and rewarding art form to the craftsman of tomorrow.

A Personal Statement

In my work there is deep concern for the materials as specific means toward expressive ends. Each material has its unique potential and it is this which I consciously and constantly explore.

The material is only the matter, the means toward an expressive, personal aesthetic end. Exploring the material and discovering its unique potential, giving it his inevitable stamp is the main objective of the artist. With this consideration he is giving form to experience, personal interpretation to a world seen through his eyes or deeply sensed in other ways. In this pursuit, if he succeeds, he adds to the experience of his fellow men who thereby see the world in a different way.

Most of my work explores the potentials of transparency. In enameling I find the possibilities of transparent color mixture endless. The changing color of the metal seen through overlays of transparents is a constant challenge. This feeling has carried over into my work with fabric and thread, and for me the most stimulating encounters in stitchery are found in the use of sheer overlays and networks of thread which create another kind of transparency.

My work in fabric and thread is conceived in terms of the material and what it can achieve in different combinations. My work is never preconceived or planned in another medium. I do not make sketches or paintings as early stages of the work, nor have I ever translated a previously done painting into the medium of stitchery. All decisions are made with the material being used. Cut shapes are manipulated and arranged, various threads are laid in with a variety of techniques and stitches, areas are veiled with nets and sheer fabrics to achieve effects possible only through these means. The completion of the work is a labor of countless readjustments made from the new relationships achieved through each shape, each color, each overlay, each stitch.

If my work has meaning or gives joy to others, I have achieved my goal—to say something personal about my world which someone else may share because he recognizes in it something of his world— the world of his senses or of his feelings.

NIK KREVITSKY
Tucson, Arizona
January, 1966

1
A Frame of Reference

Working with thread, fabric, and needle has been going on for untold centuries. There is reason to believe that man has been involved in stitching since the invention of the needle, whose original purpose probably was the assembly of non-woven fabrics into a larger, more useful object. Sewing animal skins together to form a garment or a protective covering may have been the first use of the needle in its most primitive state. We have records showing early embroidery where the actual examples are no longer extant. The earliest paintings showing garmented men indicate embellishment with embroidery. Embroidered works are depicted in ancient tomb paintings, and embroidery is alluded to in our earliest

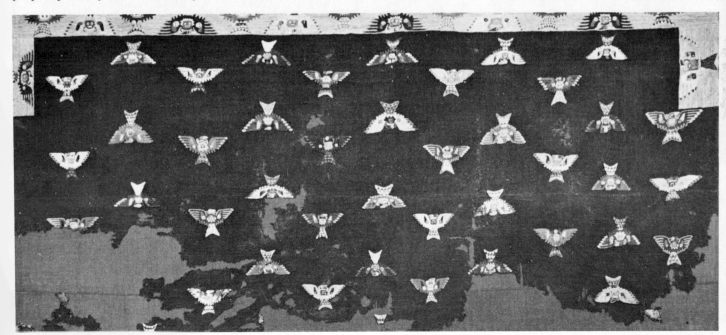

Paracas embroidery. Peru. (Courtesy Andre Emmerich, Inc.)

literature, but we have yet to discover the origin of the art of stitchery, or of the needle which made possible this sophisticated craft.

Stitched works in excellent preservation still exist from Peruvian art before the time of Christ. Many rare embroideries, including Coptic textiles of the Roman occupation of Egypt, are in museum collections today. Precious bits from the Viking burial ships of Scandinavia—preserved in the mud which sealed them at the time of burial—show unusually fine work. Early Vedic tales refer to stitching in India, and great varieties of needlework have been done there and in neighboring countries in continuing crafts traditions of recent centuries. Prehistoric American

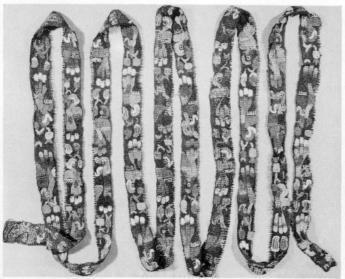

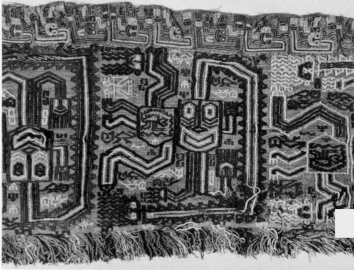

Embroidered ribbon. Peru, Nazca culture, 4-8th centuries A.D. (Courtesy The Cooper Union Museum, New York.)

Coptic embroidery. Egypt, 4th century A.D. Winged figure garment decoration. Wool split stitch on natural linen cloth (Courtesy The Cooper Union Museum, New York.)

Paracas embroidery. Peru, Nazca culture, c.500 A.D. (Courtesy The Cooper Union Museum, New York.)

Kalaga, Buddhist representation. Burma, 18th century. Embroidery with gold thread, spangles, beads on appliqué .pattern. (Courtesy Museum of Asiatic Art, Amsterdam.)

10

Indian fragments attest to an early use of decoration with thread in North America. Northwest coast Indians used appliqué and button decoration, Plains tribes used quills and beads. Middle European folk artists have done elaborately embroidered garments, and Greek island work is unsurpassed in technique. Appliqué reached a high degree of individuality in the molas of the Cuna Indians of San Blas, Panama.

Needle arts are known throughout the world. Through the centuries they have undergone little change, development, or variation until recently. In some places where continuity was lost (Denmark in particular), these arts have recently been revived with strong emphasis on

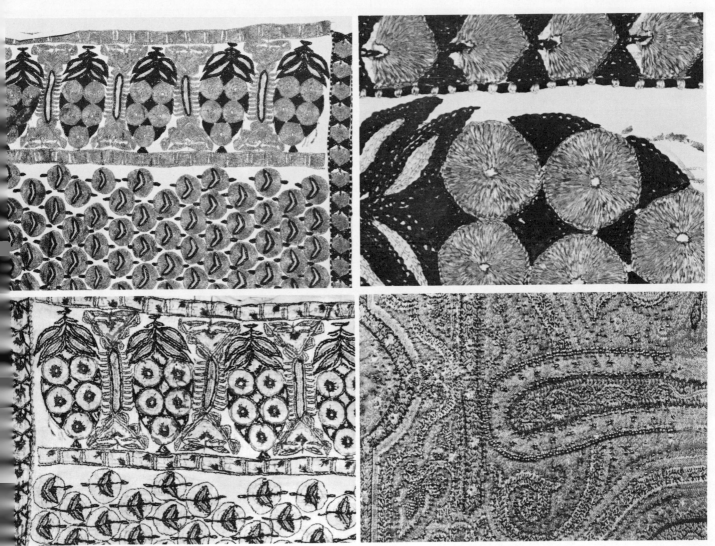

Cutch embroidery. India, 19th century.

Detail showing the combination of surface satin, stem stitch, chain stitch, closed herringbone, and whip stitch with couching on the borders.

Paisley shawl. Kashmir, 19th century. Embellished with steel cut beads.

Reverse side showing effect of stitches.

11

conventional techniques applied to contemporary design.

Traditionally called embroidery, and still referred to as such, needlework in its free and expanded state, and with its infinite experimentation, has now adopted the more inclusive term of *stitchery*.

The use of the term stitchery, which seems new though it can be found in Shakespeare, has somehow invested needlework arts with a new feeling, a freshness, a spontaneity, and a vitality.

However, the word is not the thing in this art form, or in any other. Calling a work a stitchery rather than an embroidery will not necessarily give it either a new look or any distinction it does not in itself bear.

Silk on cotton embroidery. Punjab, 19th century.

Crewel embroidered fabric. India, 19th century. Fabric completely covered with chain stitch in wool.

Above right: Detail showing mica mirrors.

Opposite: Phul Kari work using native dyes. Punjab, 19th century.

12

Traditional approaches and the continuance of pure techniques—such as needlepoint and count-thread work and many folk styles—should probably still be called embroidery. These, too, can be art and craft, as they have been for centuries.

However, embroidery is more likely than the more creative approach to fall into that no-man's land of being a busy-work pastime for the amateur who has not grown up in a crafts tradition handed down from generation to generation. Many

non-professionals engage themselves with the time-consuming activity of filling in preprinted or stamped examples, often of poor design, merely for the purpose of having something to do, with the objective of making decorative end-products for

Spanish woollen textile. 18th century. Detail below.

Greek island embroidery panel. 19th century. Typical East European folk technique.

Mola of San Blas, Panama. Appliqué shows unique slit technique revealing sandwiched layers of colored fabric.

use. This is quite different from the folk craftsman's natural feeling for the material, which he has learned from his elders. The continuance of stamped patterns attests to a need on the part of millions to be involved in the hand arts.

Periodically there have been reactions against prefabricated designs. One high point of rebellion in recent years came as a result of the industrial revolution, the effect of which was seen in the hand-work done as a protest against the machine and

machine-inspired conformity. This led at one point to the quaint erratic designs of crazy quilts with helter-skelter arrangement, perfect examples of needlework abuse, cherished today for their quaint sentimentality.

Head cloth. Guatemalan, 20th century.

Mola from San Blas, Panama. Appliqué technique shows design simplification of bird, animal, and human forms.

Cross-stitched quexquemel. Oaxaca, Mexico, contemporary.

Detail of mola from San Blas, Panama.

As an art form, needlework has presented us with many superb records, one of the most celebrated being the well-preserved Bayeux Tapestry, which is not a tapestry in the true sense, since it is not woven in tapestry techniques. It is, instead, a stitched panorama in needlework on a linen ground, over 230 feet long. The Bayeux Tapestry is remarkable for its technique, its graphic organization, and its direct recording of the events of the Norman conquest of England. It is indeed an historical document of unusual information and probably of some accuracy, since it was created soon after the event, almost 900 years ago.

The arts of the needle cannot remain

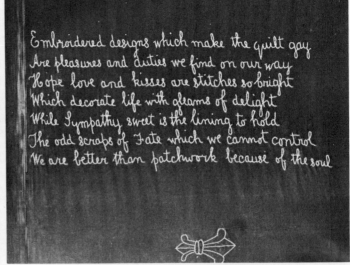

Scraps that are sombre and scraps that are gay
All put together in a fantastic way
Colors in contrast and shapes that are queer
Silk, satin, velvet, and plush are all here
Demented Fancy in gorgeous array
Rivals the rainbow in brilliant display
Such are the quilts we call "crazy" to day

Embroidered designs which make the quilt gay
Are pleasures and duties we find on our way
Hope love and kisses are stitches so bright
Which decorate life with gleams of delight
While Sympathy sweet is the lining to hold
The odd scraps of Fate which we cannot control
We are better than patchwork because of the soul

MARE

Detail, back of crazy quilt. American, 1890. (Courtesy of Mrs. D. B. Wesson and Rosequist Galleries, Tucson.)

Detail of Cottondale crazy quilt. (Courtesy of Mrs. D. B. Wesson and Rosequist Galleries, Tucson.)

Detail of Bayeux Tapestry. French, 11th century. (Courtesy French Government Tourist Office, New York.)

17

unchanged. Like arts and crafts in other media, the works with fiber, thread, and fabric have recently undergone considerable metamorphosis due to developments in available material as well as attitudes of the artists and the growing public interest in the fresh revitalized craft. Changes are forced as much by the unavailability of the traditional materials as they are by the attitude of discovery and invention.

There is a wealth of new material available to the person interested in the arts of the needle. New fibers, synthetics, non-woven fabrics, new transparents, non-tarnish metallics, and other stimulating materials are now available. A feeling that anything may be tried in the experimental stage of working with the medium has released the contemporary artist, amateur as well as professional, to approach work in needle, thread, and fabric, with a fresh vitality. Contemporary needlework has all the vigor and potential of the other graphic and plastic media, and is undergoing the same degree of innovation and experimentation they are. If weaving can emerge today as *the woven form* in three dimensions, why not carry a work in related material in the same direction? Why not three-dimensional stitcheries? Many artists are experimenting in padded forms, relief designs, suspended three-dimensional objects, intricate needle lace, and combined forms.

Stitchery can be as meaningful, as evocative, as mysterious as painting, sculpture, assemblage, collage, and the varied combinations of these. It is as legitimate a medium for expressive art as any other. At a time when all the arts are undergoing extensive broadening, overlapping, discovery of new forms, making new combinations applied to different uses; at a time when the most consistent and obvious thing about the world is change, it is not surprising to

find an attitude of innovation pervading the needle arts. Some designers are working three-dimensionally with stitchery; some are using the sewing machine with daring invention; some have explored the concept of veiling or transparency with remarkable painterly effect; others are doing unusual things with what is often sincerely called "painting with thread." Only the purist can object to this appellation of thread pictures, since many stitcheries created with the same attitudes as paintings are intended to be more than merely decorative pieces. They are intended to be evocative, meaningful expressive works, whose use, like that of other so-called non-utilitarian art, is to create meaning and feeling in the intellectual and emotional response of the observer.

Certainly "painting with thread" (if that were the whole intention of the artist) could easily end up with an imitative quality of little significance or value. We have all seen, and many have often admired, illustrative thread paintings, among the most obvious examples of which are the sentimental pictures we have inherited from the nineteenth century, and the representational decorations of the Orient. We have also seen paintings carefully copied in thread. There is nothing more distasteful than the currently available needlepoint rendition of *Blue Boy* or its companion *Pinkie* or, worse yet, *The Last Supper* reproduced as literally as possible from the original paintings. However, the contemporary artist often uses thread in a painterly fashion. When his designs are conceived in terms of thread, he cannot be accused of translating a painting into embroidery techniques.

The creative individual working with fiber and fabric does his design in terms of the material, and, after knowing the potential of it for its own expressive end, approaches his conception for a work with

the material itself without resorting to another medium for the beginning design or arrangement. In many instances the sketch is made in the same material. The method of working in other media may be related, but this approach is not necessarily an aid, unless the artist is already competent in the use of thread and aware of the basic differences between a pencil or ink drawing (or painting) and a thread drawing. He must be able to translate rather than duplicate. He must always keep in mind the basic differences; a thread work has the actuality of the thread as a raised object on the surface of the material, changing as the light plays upon it. This is quite different from the illusory effect of a graphic design in pencil, ink, paint. Perhaps stitchery has a closer affinity to collage or to sculpture in low relief when we think of it in these terms. But there are even greater differences here. Needlework is graphic, linear, and has the potential of building line upon line until all forms of great depth are created. What must always be kept in mind in working in stitchery is that thread design, no matter what we call it, is unique, has its own *raison d'etre*, and preparation for it must be made in its own terms, not those of other media which obviously, by the same token, have their own uniquenesses which must also be respected.

Needlework, like any other medium, seems to lose its uniqueness when it is imitative. We are constantly finding new combinations, new images, and we often find it difficult to give these new concepts names. The latest trends and experiment included in this publication will eventual find some kind of specific pigeonholes. Meanwhile, we see them as personal signatures of the inventive creative artist who produced them, and we include them in the broad general category of *stitchery* for the time being.

2
Recent Interest in Stitchery

The developments in contemporary stitchery may be seen as a revival of interest in the arts of needlework and appliqué and they may also be seen in relation to the general renaissance of crafts. The tremendous post-war growth in art in general and in crafts in particular may be attributed to many things in contemporary living, one of which is increased leisure time and preparation for more in the near future as a result of automation and other time-saving innovations taking place in our society.

Emphasis on crafts in home magazines as well as books may also have had some bearing on the revival. The growth of the American Craftsmen's Council and its recent establishment of a Museum of Contemporary Crafts played a great part in the increased interest and support of current activity and trends in the hand arts. This organization, now affiliated with the newly formed World Crafts Council, is doing much toward raising standards in crafts and recognizing achievements. *Craft Horizons* magazine, the voice of

the American Craftsmen's Council, has been at the forefront of world-wide activity and has brought the latest developments, the avant-garde activity in the field, to the attention of its readers. Other art magazines have begun to recognize the importance of the crafts and this, too, has extended the sphere of the needle arts.

For teachers and students the school publications *Arts and Activities* and *School Arts* have given extensive coverage to crafts, acknowledging the need for and growth in crafts in the schools. They have devoted considerable space in recent years to the subject of stitchery, and have thereby been instrumental in the recent burst of activity of this medium in the schools. Commercial companies producing materials for the craft have recently begun to prepare helpful literature and conveniently packaged material for classroom use.

If there is any one significant impetus for a revival in needlework in America and the initiating of a creative attitude, perhaps it can be seen in the work of the

late Mariska Karasz, who popularized contemporary needlework through her book *Adventures in Stitches*, published in 1949 (and revised in 1959) ; through being recognized by exhibitions in one of New York's prominent art galleries; and through a series of articles for *House Beautiful* magazine, reaching a wide circle of readers interested in crafts. Mariska Karasz produced hangings of taste and subtlety, most of them derived from design themes in nature. Her ability to use traditional needlework techniques with a fresh attitude was in no small part an incentive to many other artists ready for exploration with this medium.

Three examples of Mariska Karasz' work are reproduced in this chapter. They remain distinctive and recognizable despite many imitators. In retrospect she now represents both a link with the past and a bold break from it. Her successors have gone on into far greater inventive fields and are creating a new image in needlework arts, grateful for Mariska Karasz' contribution and her strong part in reviving a fine art form.

Square Rigged, detail. 1953.

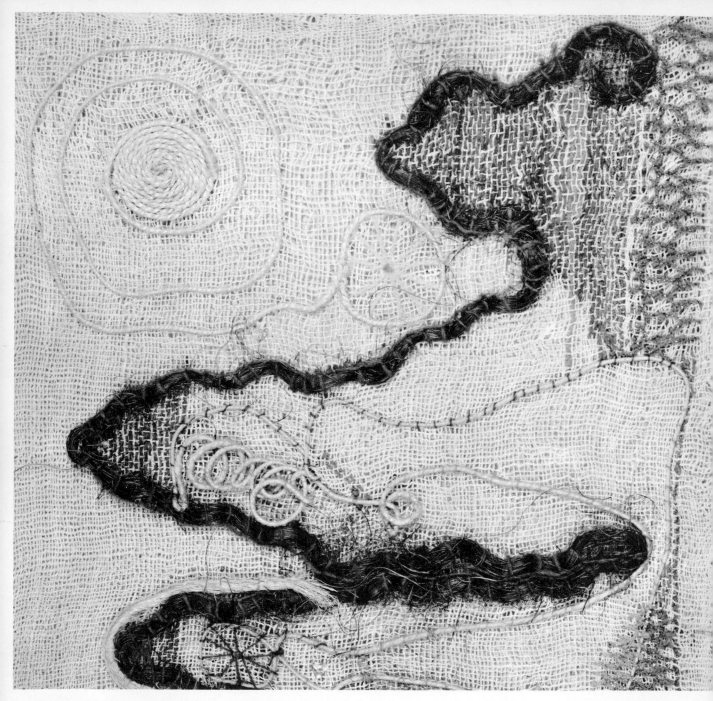

Sunday, detail. Guatemalan wash cloth with Mexican strings. (Courtesy Bertha Schaefer Gallery.)

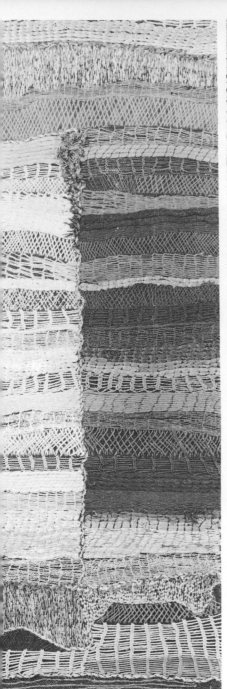

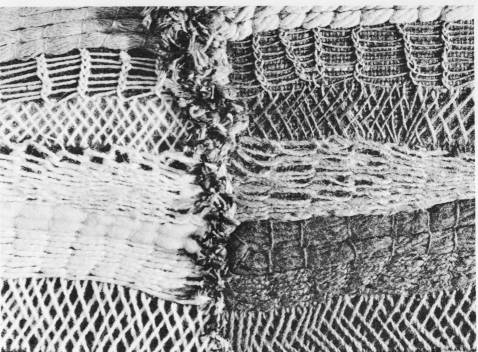

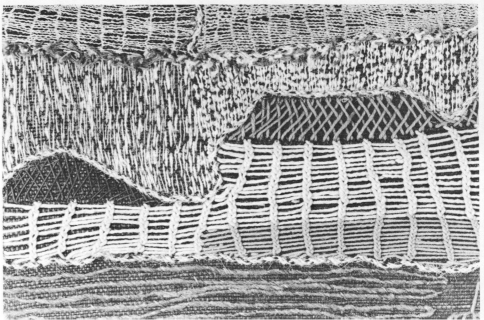

Strata. 1957. Rich browns and whites. (Collection, Estate of Mr. and Mrs. Charles Choate, Tucson, Arizona.)

Strata, details.

Votive board. Huichol Indians, Mexico, contemporary.
Wool yarn pressed into beeswax-coated hardboard.

3
Ways of Beginning

There are many ways of beginning in needle arts and it is an intention of this book to suggest a broad variety, hoping that the reader will accept this attitude and that each in his own way will find his own special technique, having discovered it for himself. Adult beginners, like children, find a great joy in feeling they have invented a stitch or a combination of stitches that is uniquely theirs. It may be an old tried-and-true basic stitch or one of its common variations or combinations, but to the person who has found it for himself by the investigative process of trial and success, rather than following some step-by-step directions, it is a true discovery and invention.

There are dictionaries of stitches, and many are explicit and easy to follow. There are many excellent books, including comprehensive vocabularies of embroidery. Some of these should be in the libraries of every needleworker, and they are listed in the Bibliography. They should be used for reference; they have much to contribute. However, in this book the beginner is advised first to familiarize himself with basic materials and tools, to do some investigation on his own before resorting to these very helpful assistants. This is to make him more aware of his own capacity and the ability to discover,

rather than to be overly dependent upon reference guides.

It is wise for the beginner to learn first to draw with thread, to experiment with different sizes and different kinds of thread; to use a variety of surfaces upon which to work; to find which materials feel right for his way of working and for the kinds of things he plans to do. Some materials may be too bulky, some too weak, some too light or dark; some may feel uncomfortable to the touch, some may seem unsuitable to the individual's personality.

Few beginners today can profit from making the traditional sampler of grandmother's day. Though its completion may give one a sense of achievement, the work as an end-product is likely to be a dead-end, leading only to other stereotypes or to kits, complete with coordinated yarns, allowing the purchaser no choice in color, texture, or stitch. We have gone far beyond the restricting limitation of a special canvas, a special thread and needle, a prescribed color scheme, and a limited vocabulary of stitches to use with our experiment or "sampler."

In the strict sense the sampler was often a disciplinary tool providing a conformist attitude toward a medium. Until recent years young ladies were taught to make samplers as ends in

themselves, not as means of discovery for finding ways of making stitches which might later be applied in a variety of uses for their own unique effects. The original intent of the first samplers, records of stitches as they were discovered by needleworkers as far back as the Middle Ages, was merely to put aside for future reference these new stitches as the artist found them.

The simple educational technique of learning by doing applies to all materials and media used in the crafts. In the textile arts providing the beginner with a variety of fibers and yarns might be a good way to initiate his exposure. Textile readiness through handling the materials can, by means of a series of developmental experiences, lead to a high degree of involvement and the production of a wide range of the most experimental and advanced contemporary designs.

The woven form, stitchery, knitted sculpture, fabric collage, and other assemblage techniques evolving out of structural work with one, two, or a variety of threads, all can be discovered by the student free to explore with yarn. The one who is taught to do a cross-stitch picture, or to fill in a needlepoint background is less likely to be stimulated to venture into new potentialities, his only experience being one stitch, one weight of yarn, and a repetitive exercise. The child who has made a God's Eye by twisting yarn around crossed twigs or sticks has been involved with the material and has had a feel of yarn. The child who has made a yarn picture by pasting yarn to paper or board has learned one way to control it. The child who has interwoven it on some kind of meshwork, using rigid hardware cloth, onion sacking, plastic screening, or other open-weave fabrics, has learned some basic things about the quality and use of fibers, yarn, string. He has accomplished this without the use of any tool or any frustrating skill, such as threading a needle. When he is ready for more detailed work or the use of the needle, the child may initiate its use and

God's Eye. Huichol Indians, Mexico, contemporary. Yarn wrapped around twigs combined with tassel ends.

the learning of the skill of threading it, of making definite stitches with it. The adult, too, might find such beginnings rewarding and a fresh approach.

Sewing on paper by outlining drawings, or on thin tagboard or railroad board by first making perforations, is an excellent way of initiating the student to many possibilities of stitching. The idea of a straight stitch being the shortest distance between two points might easily win the student who "can't even draw a straight line." Boys are easily intrigued with a wide variety of ways of working with yarn and are fascinated with stitchery, for some reason often taking to it with greater interest than do girls in most grades. Calling it stitchery, rather than

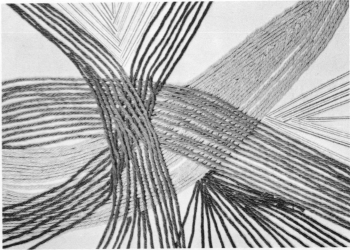

Votive board. Huichol Indian child, Mexico, contemporary. Yarn pressed into beeswax-coated hardboard.

High school student. Collage combining yarn and crumpled paper.

High school student. Collage with yarn, a preparation for stitchery.

High school student. Collage using yarn.

embroidery, helps. There is no stigma attached to or associated with the term "stitchery." It is new enough in common usage to have no negative connotations, whereas "embroidery" relates to the home handiwork of women in our culture and is likely to cause confusion if not concern in the minds of many parents, though their children might be learning many art principles through the use of so-called embroidery experiences. Traditional embroidery often leads to stilted, directed products and end results as well as an attitude of going through the uncreative filling in of another's design, although it develops skill in the technique of learning stitches and their use. The creative attitude of experimentation and

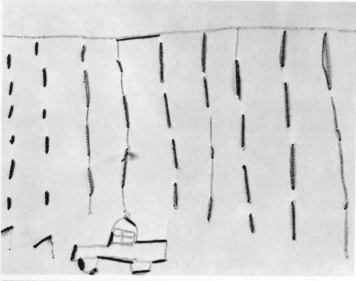

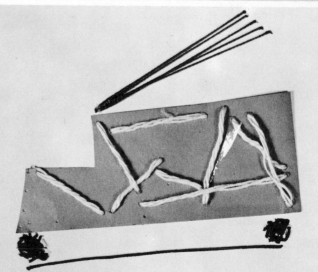

First grade. Beginning experiments with stitching on line drawing.

Primary student. Stitching on colored paper shapes.

Upper elementary student. Sophisticated stitch picture on thin tagboard.

Elementary student. Stitching combined with a cut-out paper shape.

discovery can also develop skill when skill is needed.

The period of manipulation or play with the medium should be a time in which no finished end-product is expected. An experimental piece, a kind of present-day sampler, should be attempted purely for a learning or "sketching" experience. Trying different yarns, different needles, different fabric background; combining overlays, appliqués, textile paints, felt pens, to see how they work together; trying combinations of stitches, "inventing" new ones, making a texture and color study; in other words, discovering the potential of the medium before attempting a plan for a finished end product is suggested. This is never

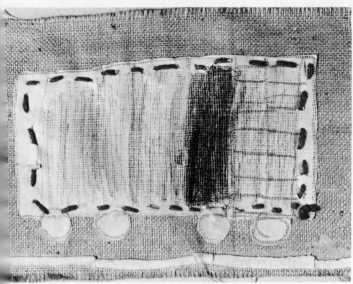

*imary student. Paper pasted and stitched to burlap, *xtured with crayon rubbing. A felt strip is pasted along *e edge.*

*rst grade student. Crayon drawing on fabric accented by *ear stitching.*

First grade student. Crayon drawing on fabric with running stitch accents.

Intermediate elementary student. Shredded yarn combined with drawing.

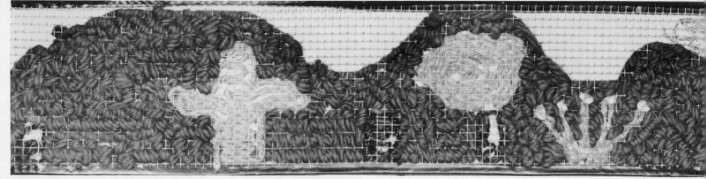

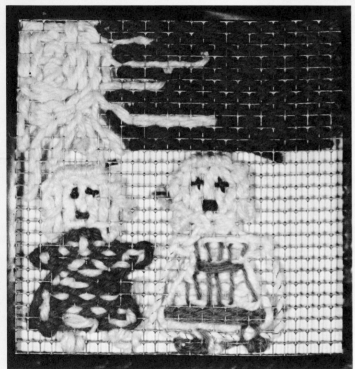

Elementary student. Stitching without a needle. Yarn picture on quarter-inch hardware cloth.

Elementary student. Stitching without a needle. Yarn painting of figures and sun; cotton rug yarn interwoven on hardware cloth.

First grade student. Yarn and fabric stitched to abaca cloth stapled to a piece of cardboard.

waste of time or material.

There is a great difference between the quality of the learning if the student is "taught" something or if he discovers it himself. Often what goes on at the investigative discovery phase of the learning experience is the most valuable part of the entire process. Through this kind of beginning the student is likely to gain a healthy respect for the work of the professional craftsman whose work he might be interested in studying or observing, or whose work he may have seen. Through this approach he might well learn art appreciation in a personal, direct way. And through this approach, if he should continue his own productive, expressive use of the medium, he is more likely to emerge with a personal statement and style.

The impatient beginner will find his first "product" difficult unless he has preceded it with exercises or discoveries, unless he has developed a feel for the medium he is using.

Elementary student. Understatement with simple long stitches creating a cityscape.

Elementary student. Bold stitch-appliqué pan

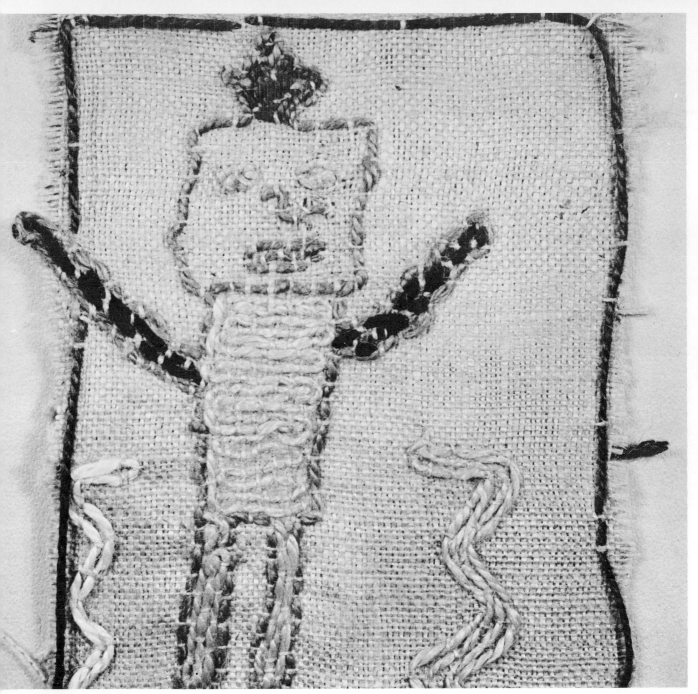

imary student. Couching effect created by running stitch through warp and weft threads of the base fabric.

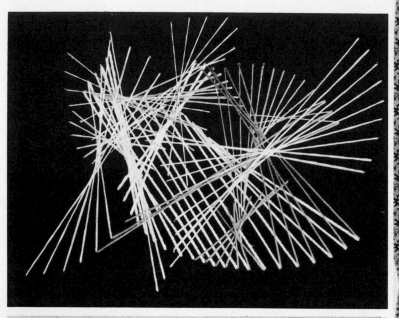

Junior high school student. Stitching on paper. Perforated holes overlap to create curves.

High school student. Still life panel using appliqué and directional thread strokes.

College level group project in art education for elementary teachers.

36

...ge level group project for elementary teachers.

Student Work

These examples show a wide range from free exploration with materials through representation, simplification, and abstraction. They are by students in San Diego, Oakland, and Denver, from fifth grade through high school.

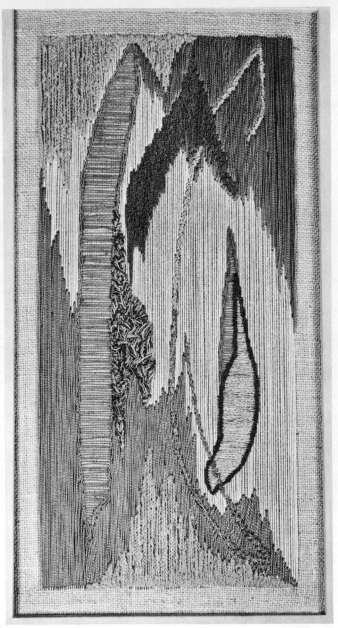

xth grade student. Simple symmetrical design on plastic rget cloth.

High school student. Restrained handling of long threads, variety of textures.

Elementary student. Stitchery on burlap with flannel accents.

Elementary student. Stitching on flimsy yet strong theatrical gauze.

Intermediate elementary student. Open work stitching on plastic mesh target cloth.

Elementary student. Stitching on stiff tarletan with accents of felt.

High school student. Lines, nets, and dots.

Perez Theresa

Junior high school student. An excellent example of subject matter adapted to medium.

Elementary student. A landscape drawn with thread.

Junior high school student. A simple, unsophisticated stitchery.

*A Variety of Animal Interpretations by Children from the
First Grade through High School.*

44

Christmas Interpreted by Sixth Grade Children.

Sixth grade student. Bold knots depict apple trees.

Fifth grade student. Excellent use of historical subject matter—a Viking ship.

Junior high school class work combined to form a group hanging. The unsophisticated expression shows a frank use of the material by teen-agers.

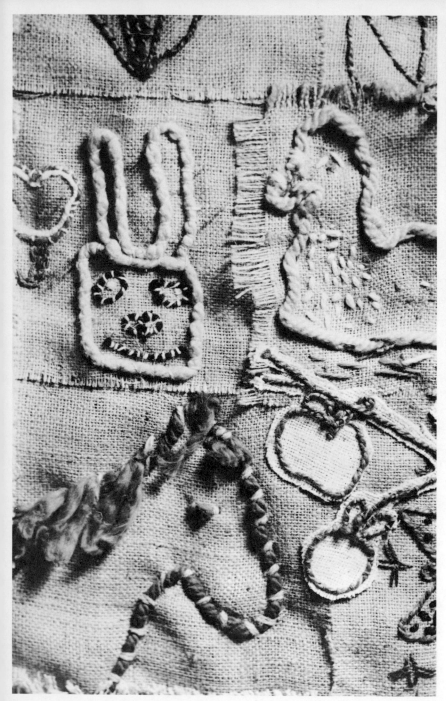

Details showing couching for outline effects.

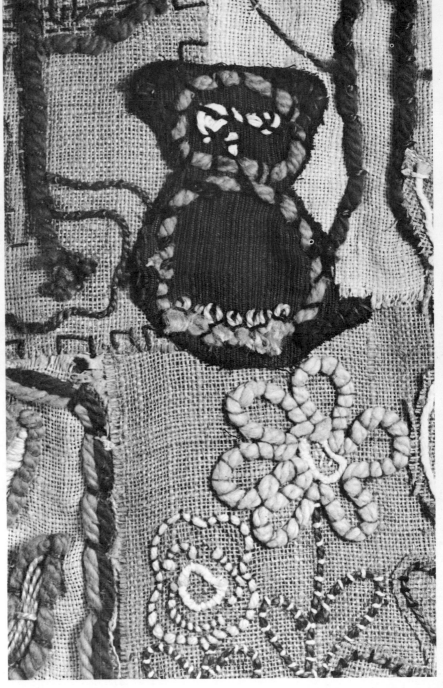

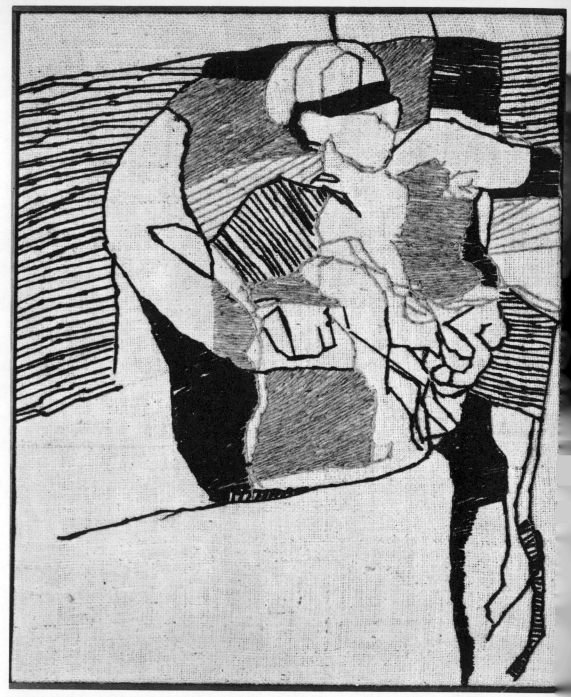

College student. A pictorial example of drawing with thread.

xamples by high-school-age students of a vocational arts and crafts school in Zagreb, ugoslavia. Technically these are highly skilled works.

Stitcheries made by young children in the mountains of Peru in a project initiated by a Peace Corps worker. The yarn pictures are stitched predominately in chain st on hand-woven wool.

Fifth grade student. Lively feeling for surface pattern.

Fifth grade student. Design fills the page.

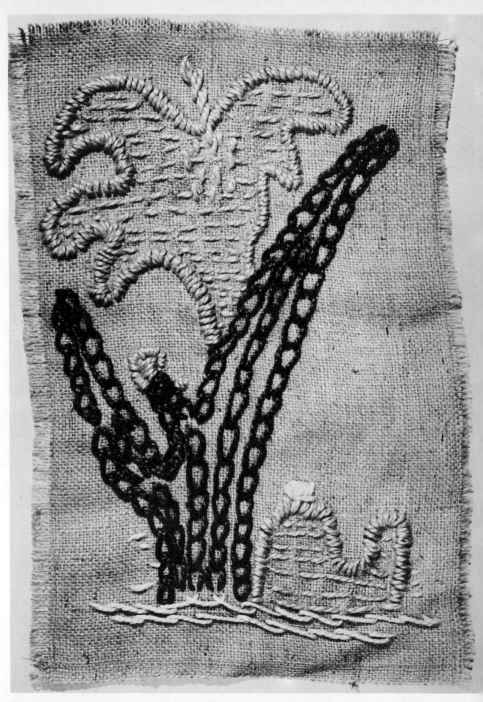

Sixth grade student. Bold use of simple stitchery vocabulary.

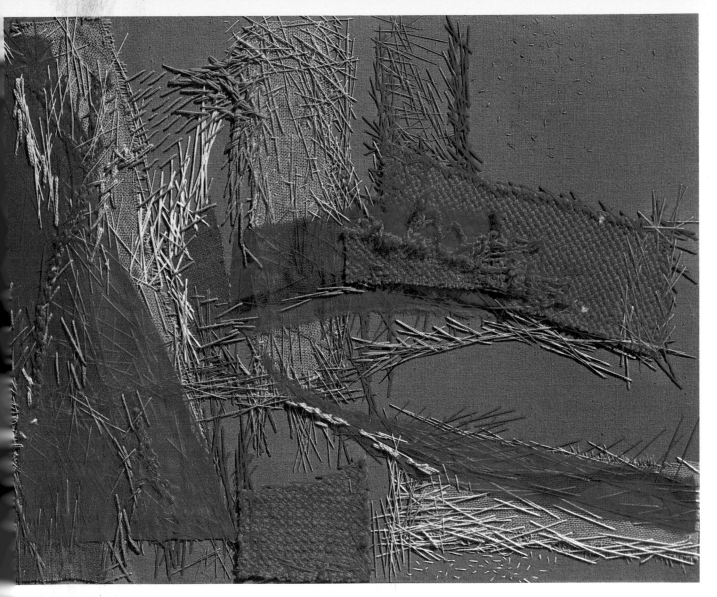

is Side Of The Snow
*e author has used the rich changing color of the fall season as the subject for an
straction of the portent of winter. A stitchery in wool, linen, and cotton with silk organza
erlays. (Photograph, Peter Balestrero.)*

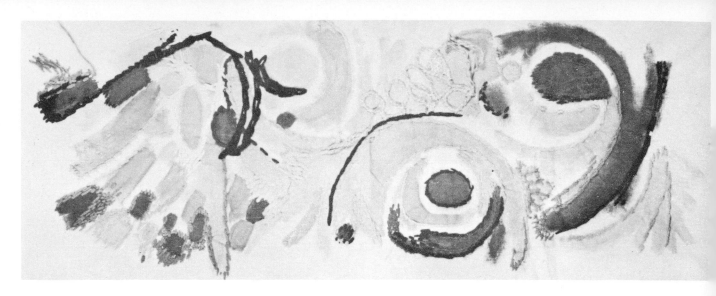

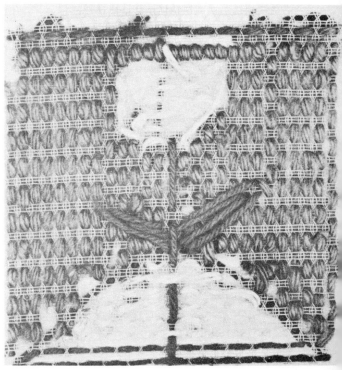

Adult. A stitchery in progress showing a combination of painting and stitch

Primary student. Pattern of plastic target cloth is incorporated into the des

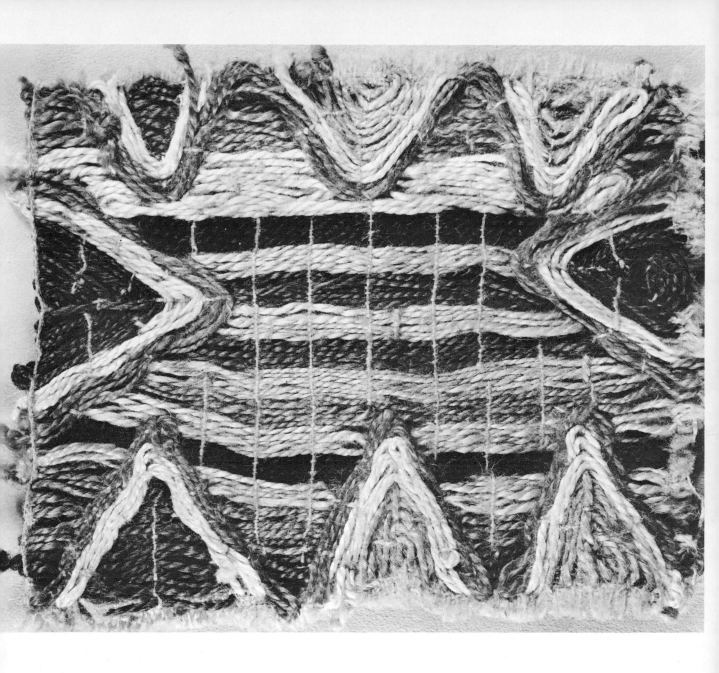

Fourth grade student. Laying the thread on the surface of the fabric. A bold interpretation related to huck towel embroidery.

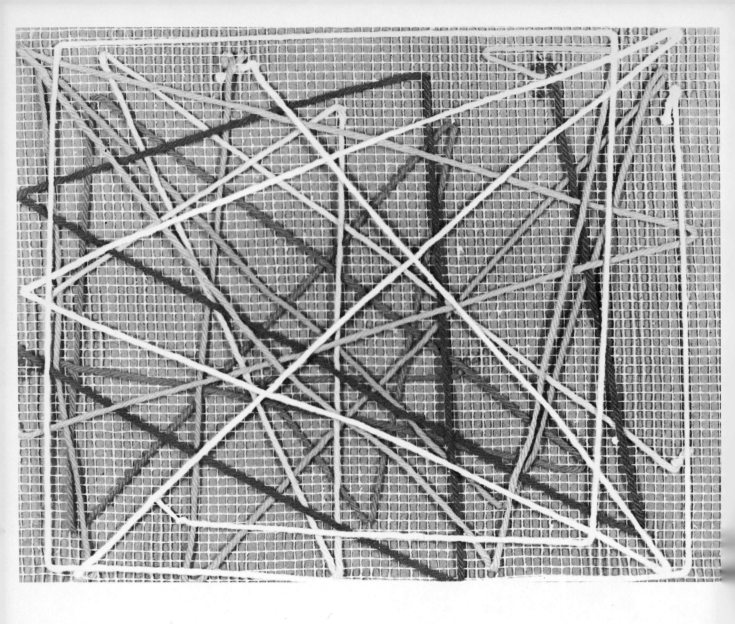

Kindergarten. Bold linear thread drawing on mesh background.

58

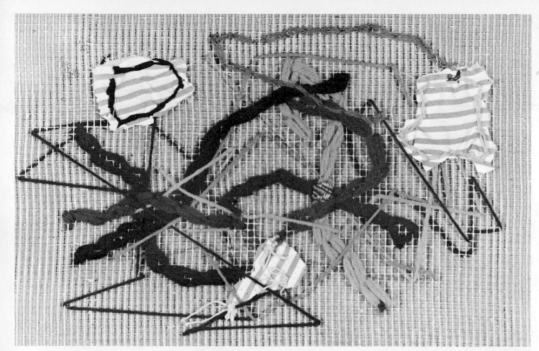

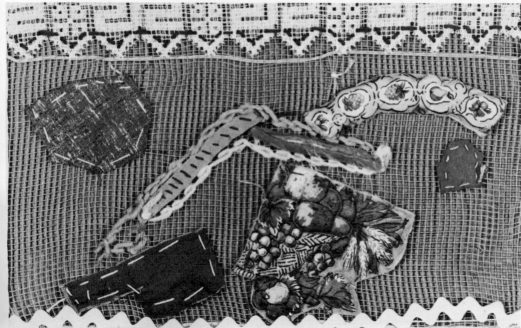

First grade. Yarn line and fabric scraps on coarse mesh.

Second grade. Wide variety of appliqué, including lace.

Stitchery by tenth grade student. Overlapping threads create the radiating quality of cactus needles.

4
Designing the Stitchery

Designing for a stitchery comes easily after one has had experience handling the materials. It is indeed difficult if the plan is conceived in terms of drawing and painting. The translation of a painting into stitchery requires considerable adjustment to the potentials of the material. If one attempts to imitate the painting he is likely to have an end product which is not representative of either painting or stitchery.

The unique qualities of stitchery, the characteristics which distinguish the "paintings with thread" from paintings with paint, are the actual textures of a variety of fabrics and fibers in combination with other materials and their changing appearance as the light plays on them. Therefore, one must think in these terms from the very beginning in designing a stitchery.

At the start one must become familiar with the feel or the "hand" of the different yarns, threads, fabrics, and fibers, and observe how they work together either in harmony or contrast for the effects desired. Certain materials might suggest a theme or a way of working. Before one can think in stitchery terms, he must know these terms.

Once used to the materials—having experimented to discover how they combine, what effects they can achieve,

what variety is possible—the stitcher is ready to adventure into a design for his first finished piece. Stitchery readiness comes from familiarity with the possibilities and the limitations of the medium. The designer soon realizes it is difficult, if not impossible, to duplicate a painting in thread.

Subject matter for stitchery can be anything; anything one sees in the real world or in the inner world of the imagination. Simplification or abstraction from the subject matter is inevitable, since the use of the needle and thread does not lend itself to detailed depiction of representational images. Non-objective designs created through the manipulation of shapes, lines, colors, and textures are usually easier for the beginning craftsman. He is not frustrated by trying to make the work look like any recognizable thing.

Nature provides us with endless themes for art expression. It is our obligation in working from its vast resources to select and simplify. Any theme can be dealt with in a wide variety of ways. We might approach a subject as seen with the naked eye, with a telescope or with a microscope.

When we use any subject for a design we must think of it only as a theme or point of departure and give it our

personal stamp, changing it by how we interpret it. The artist does not reproduce nature, he interprets it, makes his unique comment about it. The artist's work is often more satisfying to him and to his audience if the treatment leaves something to the imagination, rather than if it is so obvious that one recognizes the subject immediately and very soon loses interest in it. The challenge of the less obvious treatment and the manner in which the artist has made the subject his own expression are the things which distinguish the work and give it vitality.

In working from nature, whether it is a flower, a shell, a tree, or any other single object, we might use a variety of approaches. We may begin with the shape and develop a design by varying size, texture, color, or by arrangement or repetition. We might simplify the form by eliminating detail. We might be inspired by the color or pattern of the subject matter and select these as our theme. We might select a minute portion of the object, develop this and ignore all the rest. Our study would not necessarily depict the object that inspired it. The end product might only suggest the motivating subject material. We might be using a part to stand for the whole; we would be selecting or abstracting. A leaf may represent a tree or a forest.

The cellular structure of the leaf might also do the same.

We might well be inspired by the texture of an object and use this as a point of departure for our stitchery design. The quality or essence of a subject can be carried over into the final work. One might do a stitchery creating the strong feeling of pride through line and color representing a peacock in this way rather than depicting him in a representational manner. One can transmit the feeling a subject gives him rather than merely showing that subject as the eye sees it.

Artists also work from themes in the man-made world, from design in other fields, and from the art and artifacts of the past. One's entire visual experience is source material for his expression.

As one works he develops a sense of design, often intuitively selecting unique combinations of shape, color, texture. Some work with strong contrast, with brilliant color, violent movement; others with subtle relationships, muted tones, and a feeling of calm. We express our feelings through the kinds of materials we select for any work of art or craft. Since this is a highly personal thing, we should be given the opportunity to choose the materials ourselves, and we should have a feeling of confidence or security in our choices.

The teacher or parent should allow the child to select from a wide variety of available materials. One who makes all the choices for the student is limiting him rather than allowing him to develop his own sense of selectivity and discrimination. There are no rules to follow. The insecure individual who has to resort to a printed pattern with pre-packaged yarns to complete it is often one who was restricted in his earlier years, who may have been made to feel that his own choices would not be "right." We must remember that tastes differ and our choices or likes are not necessarily those of our students or our children. Through their experimentation new and exciting things, never dreamed of by us, will emerge.

Stifling the creativity of the young by eliminating the element of choice destroys much of the incentive in the activity. It often leads to a strong feeling of dependence and also destroys initiative. A color, a texture, a chance combination of materials might suggest a theme to the student and he might thereby be off in a wonderful world of new discovery or invention. Pre-packaged or adult-selected materials might offer him no challenge or inspiration.

Proportion and size are also important in the design. Some themes lend themselves to unusual shapes. Therefore, it is wise to allow the beginner to decide for himself also whether his stitchery is to be large or small, square or rectangular, long and narrow, or perhaps even circular. He might prefer to make a free-hanging object, or he might desire to work on a stretcher frame. He may even extend his concept into a three-dimensional form. When he is ready to plan he should be ready to make his own decisions. This phase should come after he has had time to experiment and to discover the potential of the material, after he has learned how to handle the few simple tools; after he has learned how to control the materials for the effects he wishes to achieve.

The first attempts should be doodles or scribbles with yarn and cloth, nothing more. There should be no concern for end products in the beginning experiments. Having learned that some yarns are too heavy to stitch with, or too fragile to hold up through the process of stitching in and out, the beginner might discover some other way of incorporating these yarns in his work. He might try laying them down or dropping them on the fabric and then tacking them down. Having discovered this in his experimenting, he might deliberately plan to use these yarns in the end product he designs. Having discovered that areas may be filled in with threads, or that threads on various angles create different colors because of the way they catch the light, he might incorporate this into his design. Having found many variations

of one stitch, he may design a work restricting himself to this simple but adequate vocabulary. It is not necessary to start with directions on how to make a variety of stitches. When the need arises for learning new stitches, the student can then investigate a dictionary of stitches.

Although it is more desirable to work directly with fabric and threads, it sometimes is necessary to do some planning in other media. If one is aware of the materials and can work from a sketch, he might plan with cut paper and paint. If he is using some appliqué in the design, a collage sketch might be helpful. However, it is also possible to do a sketch or small plan in the actual materials of the end product.

One of the most satisfying methods of working is to start with a ground fabric, either loose or stretched on a frame, and to arrange or manipulate shapes for the general plan, for the breaking or filling of space. One should do this after selecting his materials and the general color scheme, adding to this basic collection as the need arises in the development of the work.

In building upon previous learnings, the individual who discovers that stitching has a linear quality related to drawing, who observes that the texture of the yarn as well as of the base fabric is itself an element, and that a variety of new textures may be achieved by direction, overlapping interlocking, knotting, and other techniques has learned much about the uniqueness of the medium. If he observes color change through juxtaposition as well as through overlays of transparencies or networks, he learns color through interaction, rather than theory. Through the learning-by-doing approach the student develops a sensitivity to the proper materials for any product in the medium. Through involvement he soon learns that a painted picture, a woven tapestry, or a stitched hanging, though they all serve the same utilitarian function of providing beauty in our lives, are indeed different things and should never attempt to imitate each other.

Voodoo, by the author. Dark colors on black wool with silk and wool appliqués and yarns of mohair, wool, cotton, linen, and synthetic fabrics. (Purchase Prize, Arizona Crafts, 1964.) In form and texture there is a strong design relationship to the desert trees.

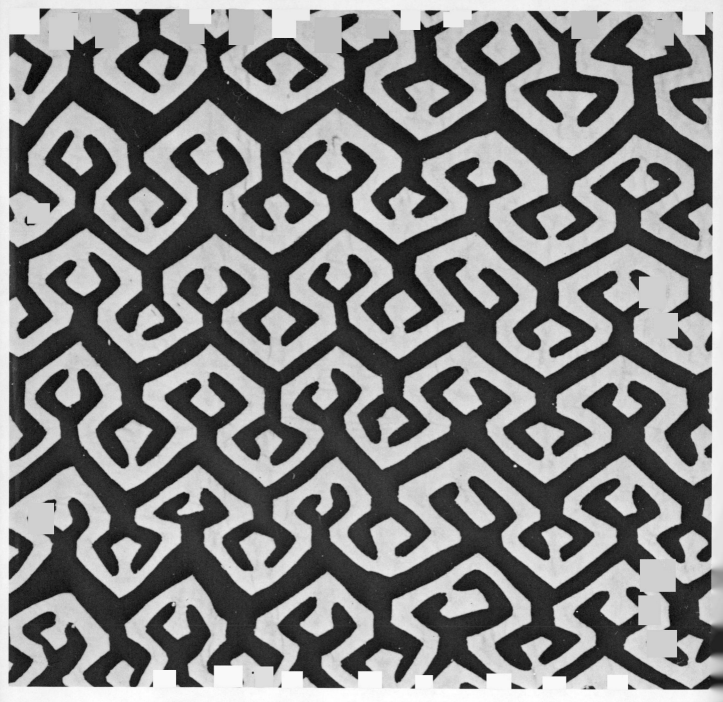

Mola appliqué. San Blas Indians, Panama. The black area is revealed by cutting through white overlay

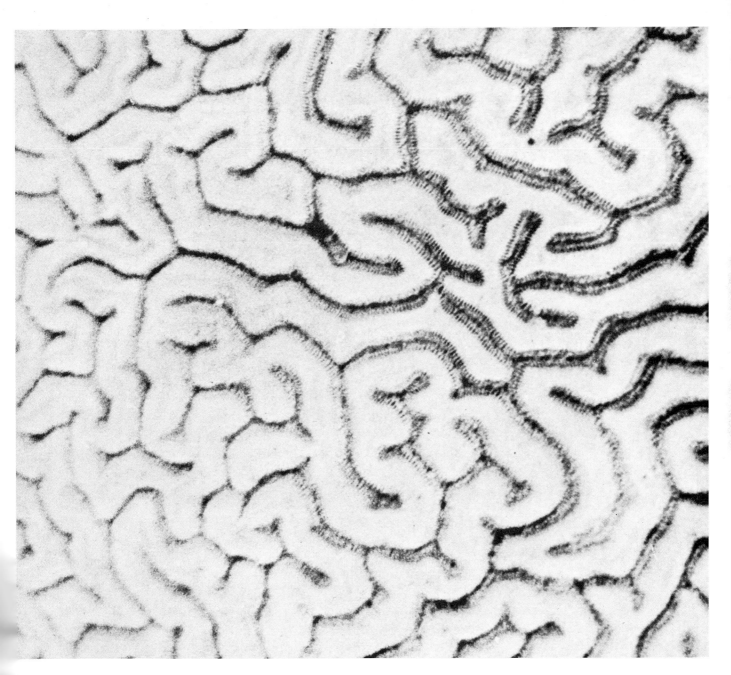

The simple pattern of the Mola relates to the design above of brain coral.

Top to bottom:
Stitchery form/microphotograph.
Radial pattern stitchery/passion
flower blossom. Stitchery
texture/lichen on rock.
Overlapped, stitched lines/
structure of Watts Towers.

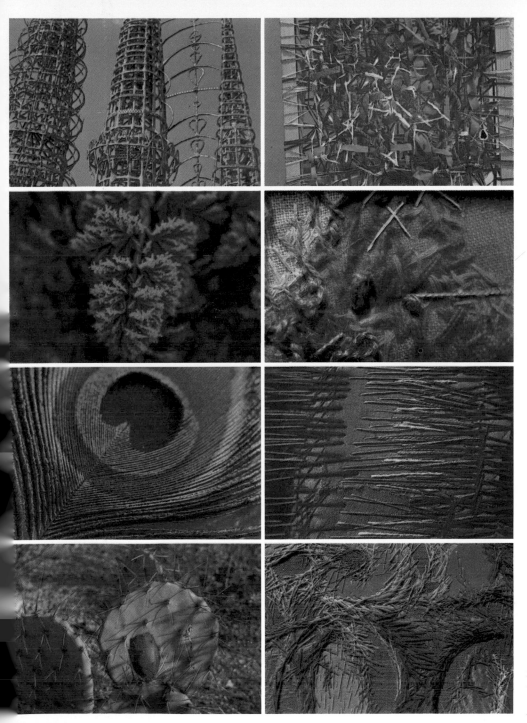

Top to bottom:
Lacy pattern of Watts Towers/
stitch experiment in open work.
Frosted leaf/stitchery
transparency. Peacock feather
eye/linear abstraction of
peacock. Cactus and fruit/
stitchery related to cactus forms.
(Photographs by Virginia
Robinson.)

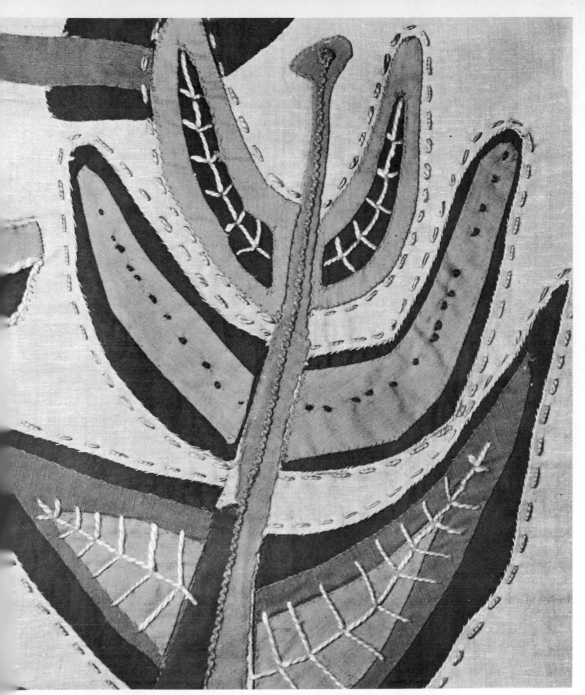

etail of hanging by Anna Ballarian. Appliqué and embroidery. The upward-reaching
ganic forms find a natural parallel in the saguaro cactus of the Arizona desert.

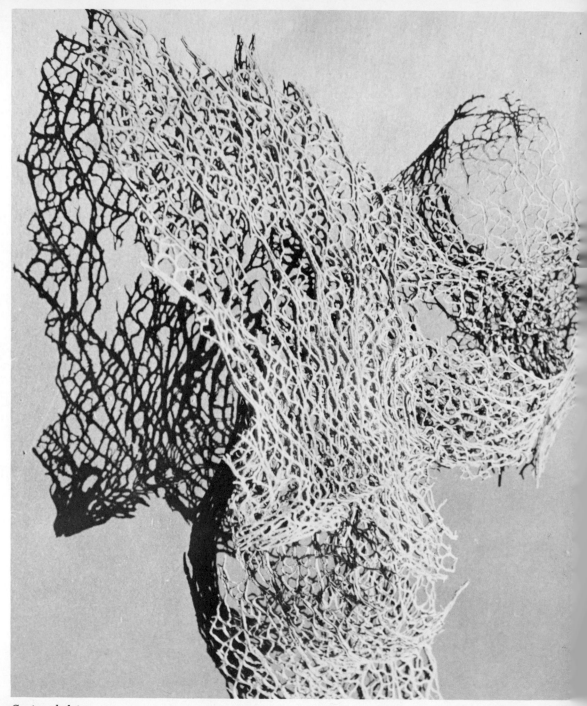

Cactus skeleton.

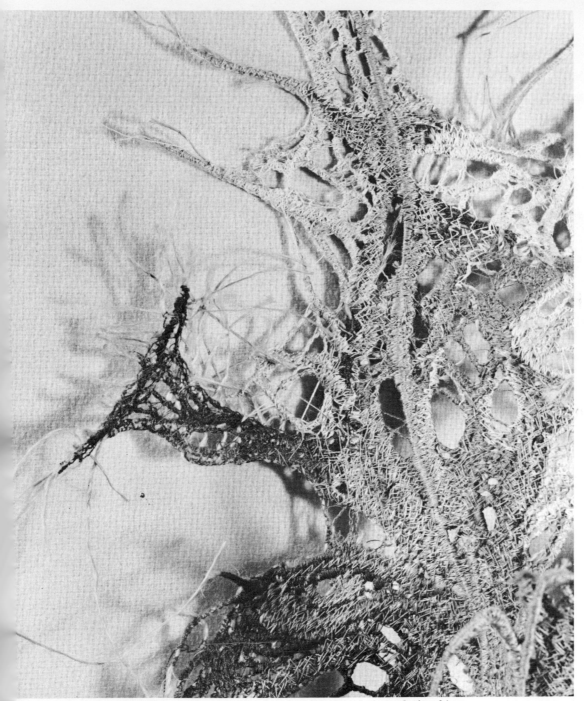

's three-dimensional stitchery by Everett Sturgeon bears a close design relationship to web-like cactus skeleton.

Trees, Sabino Canyon, Tucson. .

Fabric collage by Marie Kelly. The intertwined effect of this three-dimensional hanging relates to the overlapping branches.

izona cactus.

tail of stitchery by high school student showing stylized radiating pattern.

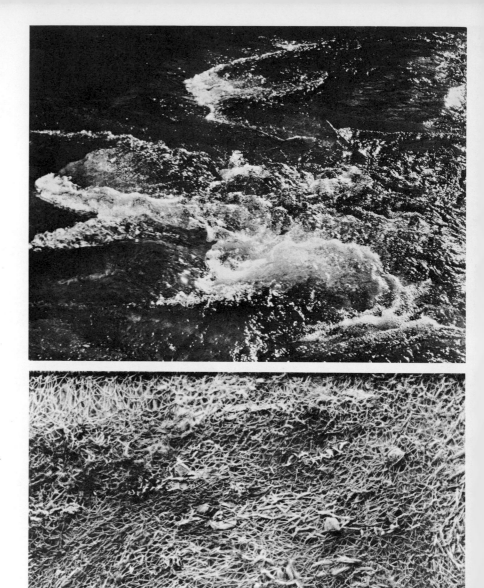

Free-hanging stitchery by Kate Auerbach relates in its dynamic pattern to the photograph of river rapids.

...chery by the author. Arched webs of overlapped radiating threads suggest rush
...ses and reflection as seen in the accompanying photo from nature.

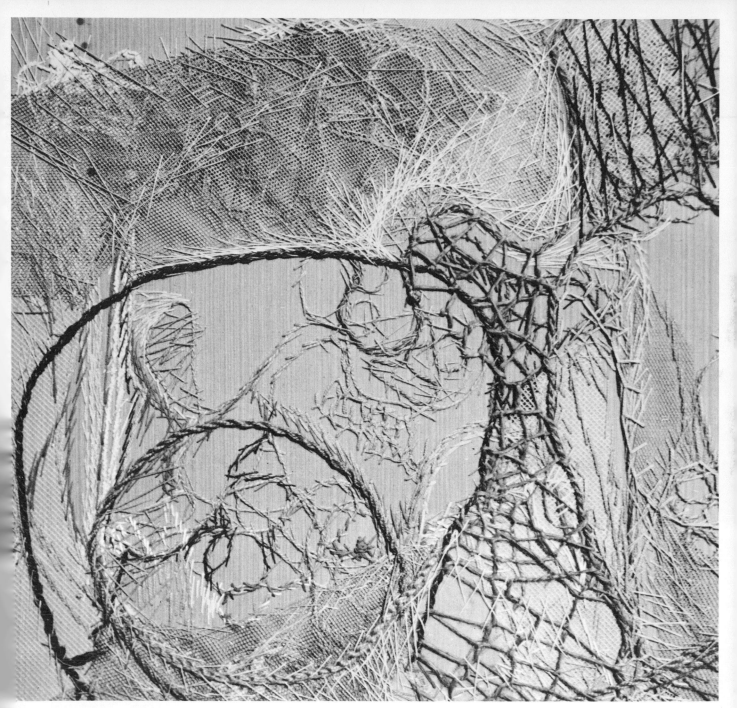

Meander by the author. Intertwining design repeats the random curves of the barbed wire.

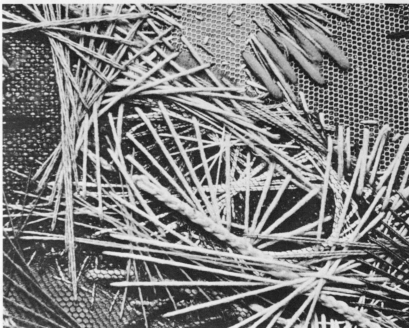

Mostly Green by the author (detail) compares in its seemingly random pattern of lines with the photograph of metal rods.

actus by the author (detail) resembles the spiky pattern
f Arizona's barrel cactus.

The author at work on a stitchery, using a large hoop.

Lotta Hagerman at work showing the manipulation of forms and the decision-making during the process of designing.

Inactive mud pools.

Sand pattern left by tides.

Charred wood.

5
The New Image . . . New Directions

Many recognized artists and teachers in the field of stitchery have been drawn to this medium after years of involvement in painting, design, and other media. For several the contemporary approach of the sheer combination of materials led naturally to a kind of fabric collage. For some who work extensively with appliqué, collage has been a direct influence. Their works relate to collage, though the purist would reserve the term "collage" for objects held together with an adhesive (since the French root "coller" means to paste), rather than with thread. The student who has had familiarity with collage can design more easily for stitchery.

New York's Museum of Contemporary Crafts in an exhibition called "Fabric Collage" showed the inventive handling of stitchery by five Americans: Lillian Elliott, Elizabeth Jennerjahn, Marie Kelly, Alma Lesch, and Marilyn Pappas. Each has a distinct style though all are closely related in the explosive period of innovation in the textile arts. Each relates directly to the kind of change going on in all the graphic and plastic arts, to what we might refer to as the new image in art. Similar experiments are being conducted throughout the world but the Americans seem to be the innovators in a fresh free look in stitchery as they were in weaving, having awakened the craft world with The Woven Form in recent years.

Anything goes in the new image—found objects, evocative bits of clothing, pop art themes, op art principles—all in the sincere searching within a revitalized medium which allows for infinite experimentation. The separation between the craftsman's work and that of other artists is becoming very narrow indeed. Works by several contemporary painters and sculptors relate very closely to the new image in stitchery. There are fabric sculpture, stitched "dolls" and string constructions exhibited in the art galleries and museums. Stitchery, as such, however, somehow continues to be shown almost exclusively in craft shops or the crafts corners of museums. Separation where it exists raises the age-old question of art and craft, a question which has been argued for centuries. Perhaps we are involved in a period of change that will erase lines of demarcation and give us a broader view without consideration of isolating cubbyholes. It is the quality of the individual work and its essence in terms of how the artist is saying what he is saying that counts.

NEW DIRECTIONS

The artist's search for form in new directions with a variety of media has led to expressive products unique to our times. Some of these works derive directly from new ways of seeing, an awareness of a universe heretofore hidden because ways of revealing it had not been found. Spacemen and unmanned rockets have brought back a new image of earth and of the heavens, and have given us the macrocosmic view. Complementary photographic developments at the other extreme have given us microscopic records. Techniques revealing the hitherto invisible insides of things have given us new experiences in color as well as form. All these means have undoubtedly given us new dimensions and have extended our language of vision. They have literally given us a new vocabulary.

The creative assemblers and organizers in the fabric media have explored the concept of transparency in a literal manner showing color mutations, value changes, and the illusion as well as the actuality of depth in their constructions. Some have also explored the psychological overtones implicit in the notion of layers or levels of experience.

Artists have been affected by the new sciences of cybernetics and bionics; they have been influenced by data processing, multi-media communication, and by atomic fission, these developments all leading to the many new art expressions which depict break-up, fragmentation, compartmentalization, isolation, and a reorganization of the complex contemporary world.

Evocative images have evolved from assemblages of materials out of context, creating powerful environments. The line constructions of Sue Fuller; the sculpture environments of Frederick Kiesler and Louise Nevelson; the woven forms of Lenore Tawney and Dominic de Mare; the three-dimensional stitcheries of Marie Kelly and Everett Sturgeon all have a moving quality related to totem and myth in early cultures. They create a feeling of combining race memory with legend stemming from today's expanded and compressed world. Baj has assembled things into whimsically frightening portraits as has Dubuffet. Marca-Relli has used fabric forms in a reassembly of cut-out shapes mounted on canvas. These are not unlike the "fabric collages" of Marilyn Pappas as shown in *Chest of Drawers* or of Alma Lesch in her *Uncle Bob* and *Mrs. Burns*. Adrienne Kraut's fur constructions and Anne Butler's pile-up are also new images which reinforce the continued invention of artists working in cloth.

Three-dimensional cloth figures

A Walk with Cézanne by Lillian Elliott. Color patch assembly. (Courtesy Museum of Contemporary Crafts.)

Passover hanging by Lillian Elliott. Bold calligraphy appliqué.

produced by contemporary artists have gone beyond the toy concept or the puppetry notion which requires manipulation by an operator to animate them or bring them into being. The meaningful work by stitchers producing three dimensionally has its own immediate and strong presence. The vitality is in the work itself, the power in its ability to create feeling thereby. The "dolls" by Irena Martens and Inge Bagge are three-dimensional stitched cloth sculptures. The rough-textured burlap figures as well as the slick vinyl people of William King also relate to this attitude. Whether they are art or craft depends upon the attitude of the observer and the culture. The difference is not one of quality; it is rather one of point of view.

Endless experimentation is going on in art classes at every level and in many parts of the world. Where an attitude of free exploration and discovery—

Appliqué and machine stitched wall hanging by Elizabeth Jennerjahn. (Courtesy American Craftsmen's Council.)

Fabric portrait by Alma Lesch. Embroidered blouse embellished with buttons on linen ground. (Courtesy American Craftsmen's Council.)

continuous exploitation of the newest materials, fresh adaptation of ever new ways of seeing—and the presentation of new subject matter are accepted new images will emerge out of the new directions which we see at present. Remembering of course that there really is nothing new under the sun we must accept these human interpretations of the universe as a persistent reiteration of man's constant search for the mystery of the world. It is hoped that in the search we remain ever grateful for art's mystery and that its magic does not get destroyed by redundancy of imagery or analayzed to the extent that it loses its individuality or its ineffability. The individual artist's signature should come through. His uniqueness should not be lost in the pre-packaged kit culture of which he is unwittingly a part.

The author's work is a case in point. Its distinguishing characteristics are the personal use of shapes, overlays, transparencies, and color. The stitcheries evolve out of the unusual Arizona vegetation, the brilliant sun, the author's individual way of seeing and his background in the arts. One's total experience funnels into each of his latest works, if these works come honestly and naturally. If they are contrived, forced, or eclectic the personality of the artist does not show through. His stamp is not there. His "signature" is missing.

Uncle Bob by Alma Lesch. An appliqué stitch portrait of blue denim jacket with objects and embroidered embellishment. (Courtesy Museum of Contemporary Crafts.)

Duenna by Marie Kelly. Hanging form with fabric and lace.

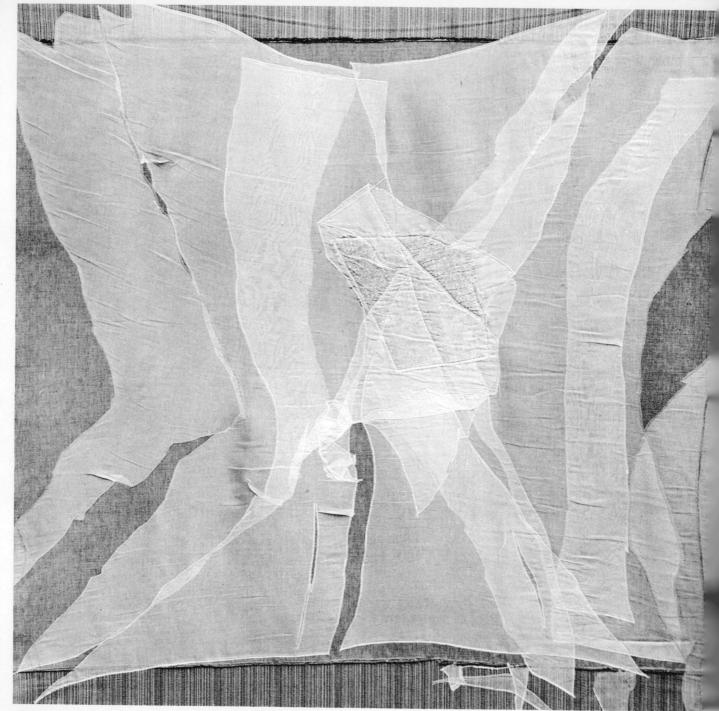

...nging form by Marie Kelly. Combines crochet net works for glass weights and open mesh areas.

...oud by Elizabeth Jennerjahn. Machine stitched appliqué panel showing use of ...rlapped transparencies. (Courtesy American Craftsmen's Council.)

Angel and Sitting Down by William King. Burlap and aluminum. (Courtesy Terry Dintenfass, Inc.)

String Composition #119 by Sue Fuller. (Courtesy Bertha Schaefer Gallery. Collection, Mr. and Mrs. Joseph Bra

String Composition #130 by Sue Fuller. (Courtesy Bertha Schaefer Gallery. Collection, Larry Aldrich Museum.)

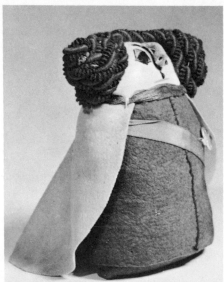

Characterizations of power by Inge Bagge.

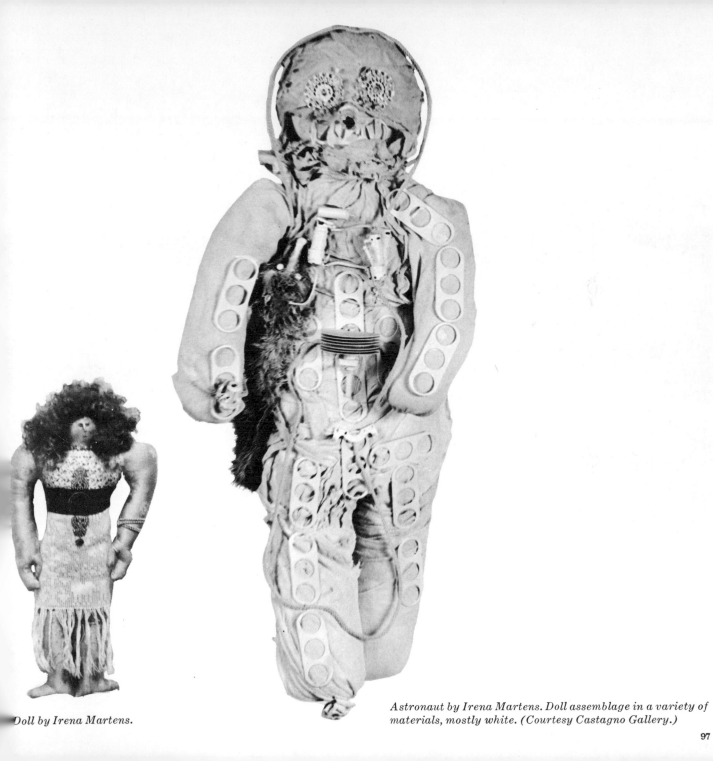

Doll by Irena Martens.

Astronaut by Irena Martens. Doll assemblage in a variety of
materials, mostly white. (Courtesy Castagno Gallery.)

97

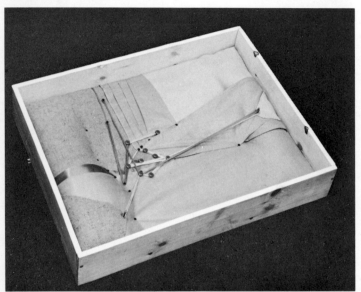

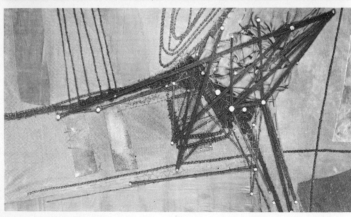

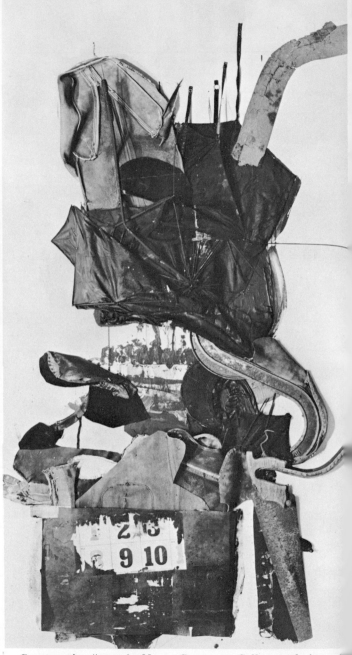

Interrupted Movement by Anne Butler. Padded form in a box, with nails, tacks, and strings.

Pile Up by Anne Butler. An experimental combination of forms.

Construction #0065 by Nancy Grossman. Collage techniques i *high relief.*

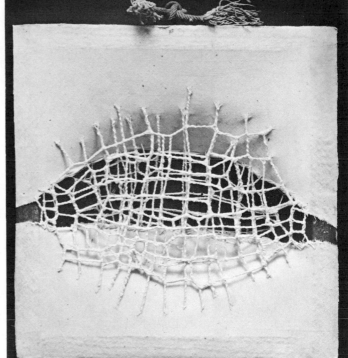

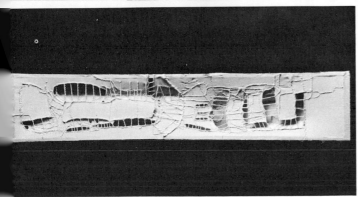

Textile collage by Inge Bagge. Bold, open-form hanging in a variety of fabrics. (Courtesy Form magazine.)

Mandolin by Marie Kelly. Use of three-dimensional concept stitchery.

Soiree by Adrienne Kraut. Rabbit hide appliqué on fake fur ground with a variety of yarns and hand stitching.

String Portrait by Marie Kelly. An evocative network cage. (Courtesy Museum of Contemporary Crafts.)

99

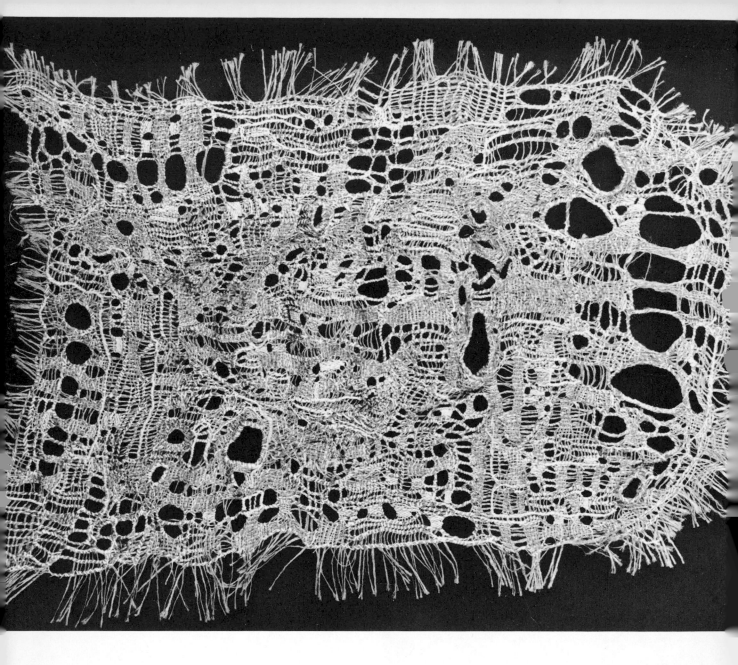

Needle lace by Marie Kelly. Stitchery, burlap, and cott

6
Gallery of Related and Combined Forms

New editions are constantly being done in the arts of the needle. Artists are today exploring stitchery with a wide variety of approaches. The urge to combine media, evident in all branches of the arts, is present. Examples of stitching over painted, printed, or screened designs; of working in open network arts; of extending threads into three-dimensional form are available in many places. The following selection of some of the new directions presents an overview of present trends. The future built on this kind of bold exploration is one of great promise for a rewarding art form.

The Village I Knew by the author.
Needle lace over fabric ground.

Embroidery by Ingrid Dessau. Needle lace hung
against ceiling. (Courtesy Form *magazine.)*

Needle lace on self framework by Kate Auerbach.

Needle lace by Luba Kréjci.

Lace construction by Luba Kréjci. Fine machine-made string. (Courtesy Museum of Contemporary Crafts.)

Detail of needle lace by Luba Kréj

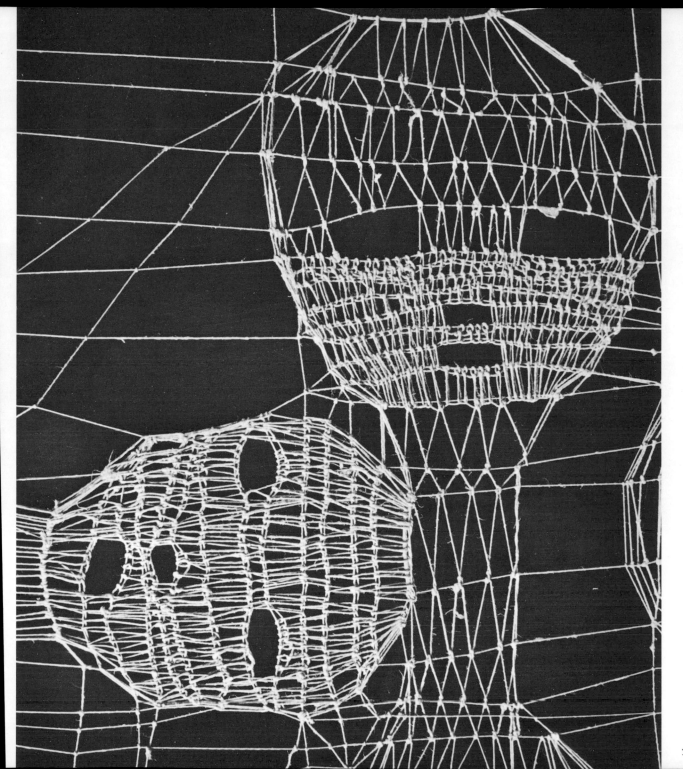

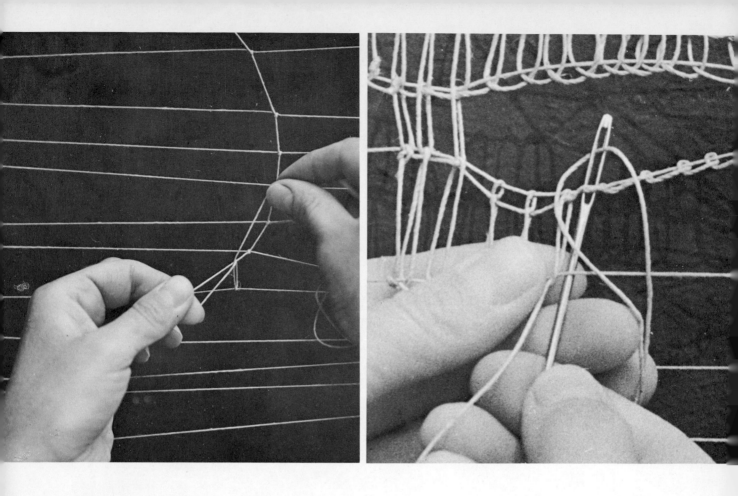

Details of needle-lace technique by Luba Kréjci.

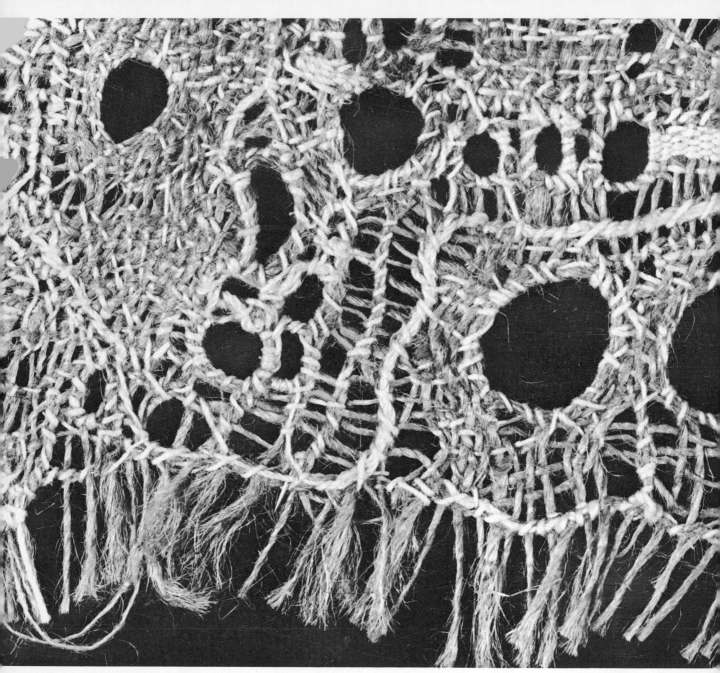

Detail of needle lace by Marie Kelly.

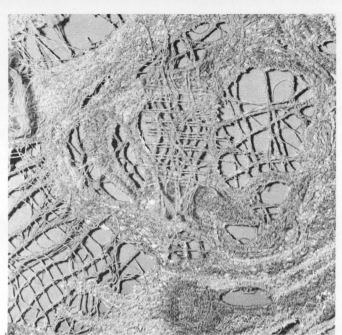

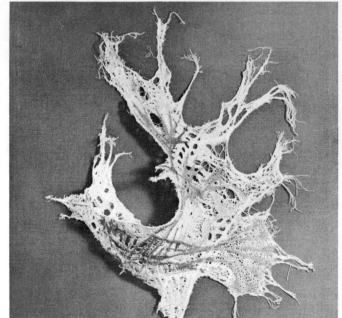

Machine needle lace by Everett Sturgeon.

Architectural hanging in Huichol god's-eye technique by Margaret Hooten.

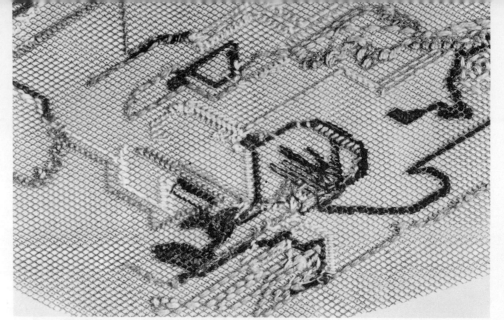

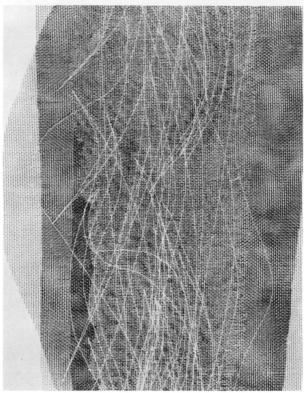

Layers of screening, machine stitched.

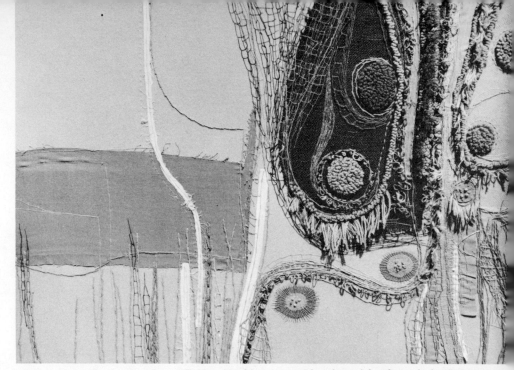

Fragments of Spring by Nancy Belfer. Hooking in combination with other stitch effects.

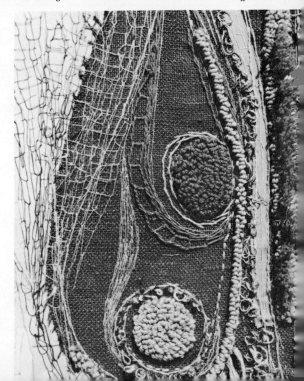

Detail of Fragments of Spring.

Wall hanging by Nancy Smith. Tufts of yarn are used for textural effect.

Hymn to Three Moons by Nancy Belfer. Hooking and stitching.

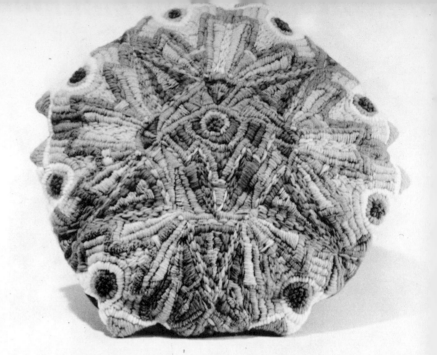

Solidly stitched pillow by Helen Bitar. (Courtesy
Henry Gallery, University of Washington.)

Composition with a Tail by David Van Dommelen.
Thread skein is incorporated in the work.

Composition by David Van Dommelen. Thread skein on surface of machine and hand stitch appliqué.

Batik with appliqué and stitched accents, including tin can mirrors, by Jodi Robbin.

Batik shapes stitched to monk's cloth ground.
Linear details in running stitch., by Jodi Robbin.

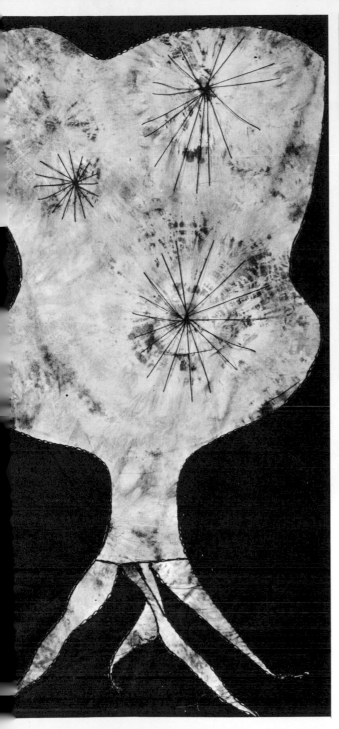

Tie-dye and stitchery by junior high school student.

Tie-dye shape appliqued to plain ground with stitched accents by high school student.

Silk screen print and cut-out collage by Zelda Strecker.

Embroidered batik wall hanging by Katherine Westphal.

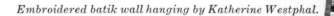

Landscape by Adrienne Kraut. Machine stitchery with raffia on canvas background.

Experimental assemblage by Claire Koller, Dade County, Florida Public Schools.
Result of work with Marilyn Pappas.

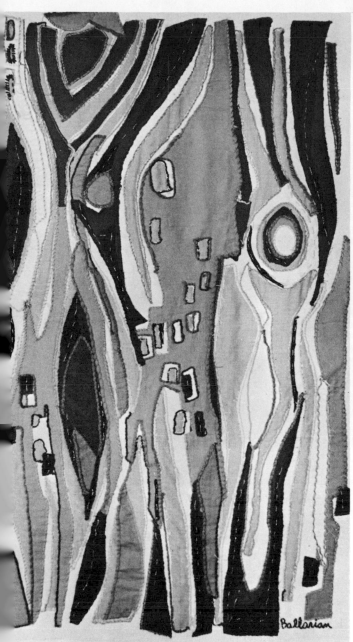

My Heart Is a Tree by Margaret Wentworth. Wide textural variety in theme and variations of leaf forms.

Appliqué and embroidery showing distinctive cording outline of forms by Anna Ballarian.

Appliqué and stitchery hanging by F. Bissiére. The effect is comparable to hanging banners. (Courtesy Stedilijke Museum, Amsterdam.)

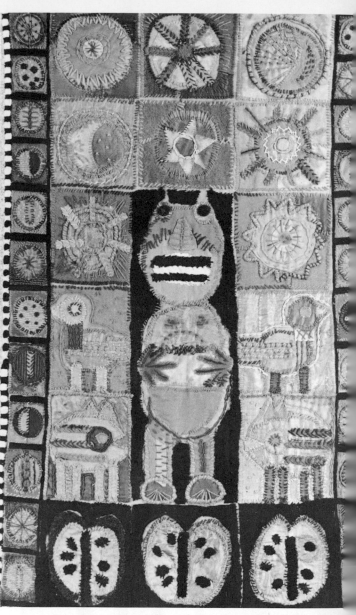

Summer by Theo Gregoor. This panel shows a patchwork approach with crazy quilt outlining of simplified forms.

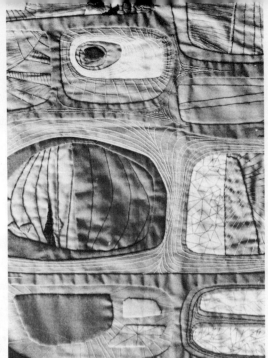

Appliqué panel by Jean Ray Laury. Adaptation of Cuna Indian mola technique. (Collection, Mary Walker Phillipp.)

ODÉ

Noah and the Ark by Charles Bodé. Appliqué and stitchery panel for child's room, showing frank use of medium for simplified design.

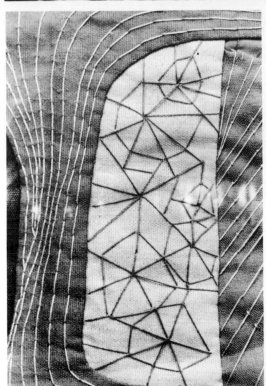

Detail.

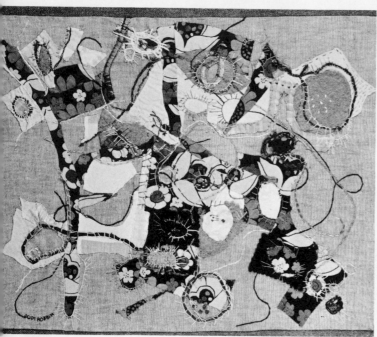

Appliqué by Jodi Robbin. Floral printed fabric combined with stitchery.

Bugs by Jodi Robbin. Appliqué of printed fabric with running stitch. Imaginative use of print.

Machine stitched appliqué game banner by Norman Laliberté.

124

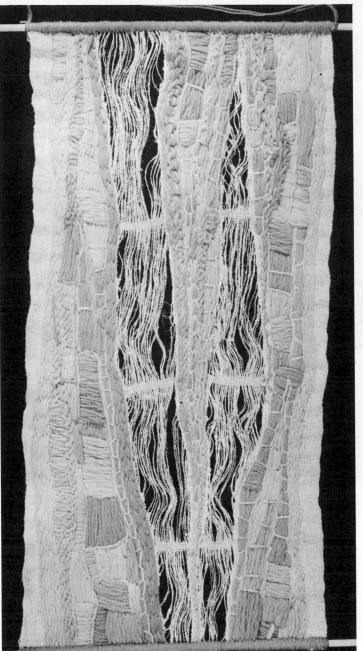

Drawn works by college students. (Courtesy Richard Proctor, University of Washington.)

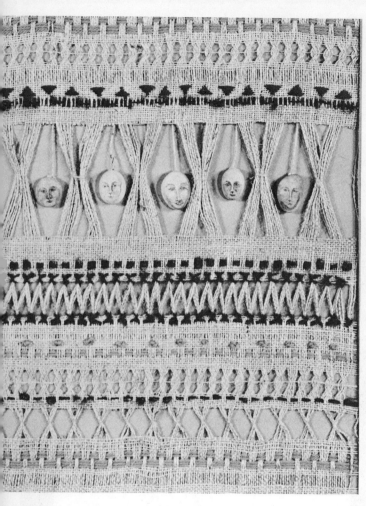

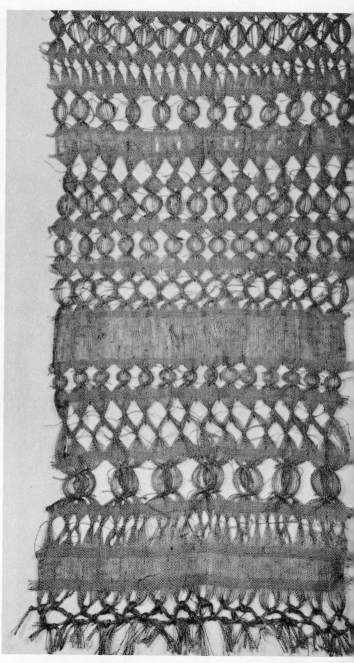

Drawn works by college students. (Courtesy Richard Proctor.

Study by Lotte Hofmann. Machine quilted embroidery with feathers. (Courtesy American Craftsmen's Council.)

Study with assorted shells hand-stitched to linen ground by Lotte Hofmann. (Courtesy American Craftsmen's Council.)

7
Tools and Materials

Needles:

Pointed End
Crewel (fine work)
Chenille (medium)
Darning 5/0-1/0
Upholstery or sail (curved)

Blunt End
Tapestry Nos. 20 to 13 (large eye)

Other Tools:
Scissors (fine pointed)
Thimble
Hoop or frame

Thread:
Household string, butcher twine,
package wrapping cord
Embroidery floss, six strand
Pearl cotton (No. 3, 5, or 8)
Crewel or rug wool
Knitting yarns
Cord
Metallic threads
Raffia
Rope
Linen, silk, jute, and synthetic
yarns (nylon and rayon)

Fabrics:
Burlap (jute)
Linen (Belgian or Peruvian)
Cotton (monk's cloth, Indianhead,
muslin)
Nets
Felt, pellon (non-woven fabrics)
Wool
Knit fabric (jersey)
Heavy upholstery
Sheer casement cloths
Tarletan, theatrical gauze, and
other nets
Daisy mesh, onion sacking
Screening (metal or plastic)
Remnants (decorator samples)
Scrap fabrics (dressmaking cuttings)
Garments (or parts of them)

Other Materials:
Fur, leather, feathers, snakeskin
Lacing (shoe laces)
Braid (binding, rick-rack)
Ribbon
Buttons
Beads
Found objects from nature (shells,
twigs, seed pods, grasses)
Anything that may be stitched or any
surface to which it may be stitched
is worth incorporating into a work
if it fits the artist's notion or
his style of working.

FABRICS
Anything that can be stitched down to
a surface is a legitimate material for
stitchery. However, the novice might
find some traditional or orthodox
materials an aid in the beginning.
A coarse or open-mesh fabric, or one in
which the warp and weft threads are
easily distinguished, works best for the
beginner. If the stitcher is concerned
with making even stitches, practice on
fabrics with woven or printed designs
might give him some security. Stitching
across stripes will allow one to control
the length of a simple running stitch.
Working on a checked fabric like gingham
will develop skill in cross-stitch or other
stitches built on a square. If one is
concerned with counting threads for
evenness of stitches, he may find the
basket weave pattern of monk's cloth
helpful. In working with heavy threads
the problem can be simplified by
creating openings in the fabric with
drawn threads. This can be done in
either the warp or the weft (or both)
of the cloth. Loose weave fabrics or
fine nets make good surfaces for the
beginner. Theatrical gauze, tarletan,
daisy mesh, plastic screening, fine mesh

hardware cloth, curtain net, buckram, and onion sacking make excellent surfaces for the person who wishes to work freely and boldly, or for the young child whose manual dexterity is not yet highly developed.

Most of these fabrics are stiff enough to use without a hoop or stretcher frame. Some precautions should be taken in their use, however. It is wise to prevent raveling by running a line of strong glue around the edges, or by fine machine stitching along all sides. Flimsy materials may be starched for easier handling. Metal screen or hardware cloth should be taped around the edges to prevent scratches or cuts. Where the openings are large enough to take heavy yarns, such as rug yarn, the stitcher might stiffen the end of the yarn with paste and then use the yarn length as he might a tipped shoe lace, going in and out without the use of the needle.

NEEDLES AND THREAD

For convenience in working, the length of the thread should be approximately the length of one's arm, or twice that if it is being used double. When the thread is too long it is likely to snag or to get worn through extensive friction while being used. Once one has learned the simple act of threading the needle, there should be no problem in having to do this often. An over-long thread is not a time-saver.

Threading the needle is not difficult if one has the proper size needle for the yarn he is using. Blunt tapestry needles with large eyes are recommended for beginners and children. These work best on loosely woven fabrics like burlap and monk's cloth. An important thing to remember is that the eye of the needle opens the fabric to allow the thread to penetrate. If the fabric is tightly woven,

whether thin or heavy, it is difficult to pull a heavy thread through it. The thread should not be forced through; it may tear the fabric. If a heavy thread is desirable, it might best be used on the surface of the cloth and held down with tacking or couching. This is especially important when using non-woven fabrics—felt, pellon, etc.

Six-strand embroidery floss or twisted pearl cotton Nos. 3, 5, or 8 are good to begin with. Fine linen, silk, and wool yarns are excellent, but not necessary for the beginner. Ordinary string or twine is adequate for beginning. Scrap yarns from any knitter's collection are usable if one learns to thread these fuzzy fibers by the simple technique of overlapping the thread on the side of the needle, slipping it off while tightly held, and inserting it, doubled, into the needle eye.

Weavers are a good source for scrap yarns. Since warp threads must be strong, warp ends are excellent to use in stitchery. A thread that tears easily must be used with extreme caution.

OTHER MATERIALS

Other recommended materials for the novice are an embroidery hoop or frame, scissors, and a thimble. These and an assortment of needles, yarns, and fabrics are all one needs to begin. Some pointed needles, such as the crewel embroidery needle, and some blunt needles, such as tapestry and rug needles, are advisable. The long-eyed chenille needle is good for some heavy yarns. Very bold work may be done with the giant size No. 10 Boye needle or with sail needles, or curved upholstery needles. The needle one selects should accommodate the thread and work easily on the fabric to which it is being attached.

Once these few simple tools and materials are assembled, the beginner is ready to stitch. He threads a needle, makes a knot at the end of the thread, brings the needle through the back of of the fabric, and is off on the adventure of making the first stitch. If the fabric is a frame or stand, the stitcher is free to use both hands. After the first stitch the work is a constant challenge. Every stitch changes the appearance of the entire work because of new relationships which develop in the on-going process. The stitch will soon discover that the tension of the thread is important. If it is pulled too tight, the entire work will pucker; if it is too loose the threads will seem to sag. If the fabric is stretched on a hoop or fram the problem of tension control is usually taken care of.

The artist is now ready to begin. All he needs is imagination, an experimental attitude, and the perseverance to carry the problem to a conclusion which satisfies him. If he finds that others enjoy it, he has succeeded beyond the expressive and personal level to that of communicati his feelings and ideas in a versatile and fresh medium.

Acknowledgments

The author is deeply indebted to many who cooperated in the production of this book. The work of many photographers was used. Without their visual presentation of the works of art the value of this book would be greatly lessened. Among the photographers are:

Hakan Alexandersson
Hazel Archer
Barton L. Attebery
Anna Ballarian
Irene B. Bayer
William Benedict
Ferdinand Boesch
Wynn Bullock
Eileen Darby
William Eng
Bill Gamble
Grover Gilchrist
Elaine Robak
Walter J. Russell
Jack Sheaffer
Still Photo Studios
John F. Waggaman
Wong and Wong

The major work is that of Virginia R. Robinson and Peter Balestrero, whose photographs of nature and examples of stitchery comprise the core of this book. For their artistry the author is most grateful.

Schools and other professional institutions have contributed much: To Aileen Webb, Paul Smith, and Renita Haufling of the American Craftsmen's Council, to LaMar Harrington of the Henry Gallery, to The Cooper Union Museum, Castagno Gallery, Andre Emmerich, Inc., *Form Magazine*, and Bertha Schaefer Gallery I extend my thanks.

The following have provided works by students in their schools: Stanley Cohen, Oakland Public Schools; Evelyn Krakover, Chicago Public Schools; Leven Leatherbury, Anne Parker, and Judy Hermanson, San Diego City Schools; Alice Hallam, San Diego County Schools; Don Allen and Elaine LaTronico, Denver Public Schools; Rosemary Beymer, Kansas City Public Schools; Richard M. Proctor, University of Washington; Louise Misto, Lee Wright, Faye Turner, Betty Toothman, and all of the other teachers of the Tucson Public Schools who contributed towards this book.

Bibliography

Pamphlets

Two invaluable aids, each illustrating and describing one hundred stitches:

Dictionary of Embroidery Stitches, 1961. *Woman's Day Magazine*—25¢
Post Office Box 1000, Department WDL
Greenwich, Connecticut 06830.

One Hundred Embroidery Stitches.
Coats and Clark's Book No. 150— $1.00
Coats and Clark's Sales Corporation
430 Park Avenue
New York, New York 10022.

Wall Chart

Basic Stitches for Creative Stitchery
Eight basic stitches, an excellent classroom visual aid available free from:
Educational Division
Lily Mills
Shelby, North Carolina.

Books

Beitler, Ethel J., *Create with Yarn*. International Textbook, Scranton, Penna., 1964.

Birrell, Verla, *The Textile Arts*. Harper and Row, New York, 1959.

Butler, Anne, *Teaching Children Embroidery*. Studio Vista, London, 1964.

Dillmont, Therese, *The Encyclopedia of Needlework*. D.M.C. Publication.

Douglass, Winsome, *Discovering Embroidery*. Taplinger Publishing Co., Inc., New York, 1962.

Enthoven, Jacqueline, *The Stitches of Creative Embroidery*. Reinhold Publishing Corporation, New York, 1964.

Hartung, Rolf, *Creative Textile Design*. Reinhold Publishing Corporation, New York, 1964.

Karasz, Mariska, *Adventures in Stitches*. Funk and Wagnall's Co., Inc., New York. Revised 1959.

King, Bucky, *Creative Canvas Embroidery*. Hearthside Press, Inc., New York, 1963.

Miller, Irene Preston and Lubell, Winifred, *The Stitchery Book; Embroidery for Beginners*. Doubleday & Co., Inc., Garden City, New York, 1965.

Schuette, Marie and Muller-Christensen, Sigrid, *The Art of Embroidery*. Frederick A. Praeger, Inc., New York, 1964.

Thomas, Mary, *Dictionary of Embroidery Stitches*. Hodder & Stoughton, London.

Van Dommelen, David B., *Decorative Wall Hangings*. Funk & Wagnall's Co., Inc., New York, 1962.

Wilson, Erica, *Crewel Embroidery*. Charles Scribner's Sons, New York, 1962.

Periodicals

Craft Horizons, American Craftsmen's Council, 44 West 53rd Street, New York, New York 10019.

Embroidery, The Embroiderer's Guild, 73 Wimpole St., London W.1; in U.S.A. 30 East 60 Street, New York, New York 10021.

Handweaver and Craftsman, 246 Fifth Avenue, New York, New York 10001.